Contents

Introduction

B lue jeans: the great equalizer, that quintessentially American garment whose history is woven throughout the world's history. From the callused-handed California gold miners to Dust Bowl migrants, from screen icons to rock stars, from socialites to Silicon Valley elites, blue jeans have been the fashion common denominator that unites the 99% and the 1%.

Whatever is your social or economic status, wearing jeans sends the message, "I'm one of you…even if I just paid $250 for this strategically shredded and faded pair of designer jeans."

There are many reasons we love them. They represent what is durable, lasting and natural. And because of their raw pedigree they represent something real as opposed to the fantasy outfits that make up much of fashion.

Jeans imply an easiness of attitude and a lack of artifice. We love their flexibility. Wearing them with a spectacular pair of heels or a simple blazer instantly elevates their status. Wearing them with a white crisp blouse makes a classic piece more hip and current. In fact wearing them with any number of the classic wardrobe pieces instantly turns them into classic too.

They can be a second skin or a form of camouflage. And of course, they're sexy. Whether we're wearing a body hugging style or boyfriend jeans we love them for what they reveal and what they don't. (A pair of boyfriend jeans suggests you actually have a boyfriend and that you're intimate enough to wear his jeans.)

Utilitarian or tailored, boyfriend or skinny, traditional color washes or candy colored, jeans are worn with confidence and enjoyment by people in all parts of the world today.

1

What Makes Jeans... Jeans?

We traditionally think of jeans as being made from denim but lately you'll see what are described as jeans in a variety of fabrics from corduroy to leather. Still, there are certain key elements that determine whether you're buying a pair of jeans or a pair of pants with some jean features. For our recommendations in this book, we'll just be referring to those made from denim. And although they come in all the colors of the rainbow, we'll only be recommending specific styles that fall into the category of blue denim. (Going into the thousands of styles and other fabrics and colors was just a little crazy making!) And although the jeans with exaggerated rips and shreds are currently (at least of this writing) wildly popular, like all things, this too shall pass. So the recommendations listed here are mostly pretty traditional. (You can shred or rip your own, of course.)

First of all, in traditional jeans there will always be some form of external rivets. These metal studs harken back to the days of the gold miners whose work clothes needed something stronger than just heavy thread to secure the seams. Next, traditional jeans always have a front seam zipper, usually metal, and a metal button, or in the case of button fly styles, a row of metal buttons. They also have multiple pockets. And finally jeans have French seams: folded over double stitched. Many also have contrast color stitching.

How jeans are made

The rugged, sturdy twill textile used to make jeans originated in the northern Italy town of Genoa, and was a staple for hardworking laborers. In fact, the fabric was so dense and sturdy that it was initially used for the sails on ships. By the mid-1800s <u>Levi Strauss and Company</u> began importing them to the US for the hard-scrabble workers in California's gold mines.

Today, the denim fabric used in jeans is manufactured by companies all over the world, including Europe (Italy and Spain), Turkey, (where more than 35% of denim comes from), South America and more recently, Mexico, and the US, but especially in the Far East (India, Pakistan, Uzbekistan, Afghanistan, Japan, China, Hong Kong, Indonesia, and Thailand).

These days, 75% of the designer jeans sold in the world are sewn in California. (No surprise there.)

Whatever the price tag, denim fabric is basically a twill textile that combines indigo dyed warp threads with undyed white weft threads. That's why when you look at the inside of your jeans the threads look white, regardless of the dye color on the outside. Unlike a lot of other fabrics, the warp threads for denim are dyed before they're woven. If the garment is designed to have some give, as in most jeans these days, there will be stretchy fibers — **spandex, elastane or Lycra** — woven in with the twill threads. Some of the higher-end manufacturers use fabric that has the stretch fiber wrapped around the twill thread, creating a very sturdy material that keeps its shape longer — and keeps your shape in check. **Rayon, a natural fiber** is becoming a popular addition — sometimes as much as 50% — in some higher end fibers because it keeps its shape so well. Some denim is pre-shrunk before it's constructed into jeans, which means they shouldn't shrink more than 3% after you wash them.

Originally the dye used to make jeans came from the indigo plant, mostly from India. But today synthetic indigo dyes are more commonly used. Depending upon the depth of color the manufacturer wants, the dye process involves dipping rope-y bunches of cotton thread into a dye bath multiple times, followed by airing out the ropes for oxidation and then repeating the process. (Many jeans 'bleed' onto lighter fabrics. A lot of synthetics hold the dye better.) That much-desired "faded" look occurs when some of the layers of indigo dye wash out during laundering. **This** is a wonderful video about indigo dye.

Then there are processes to make them look even more worn: sandblasting with pumice stones and abrading with sandpaper. That's what creates the cool "worn these forever" look. Sometimes the pumice stones are dipped in bleach or other caustic chemicals to create what's called the "acid washed" finish. Unfortunately the byproducts of this process cause health problems. Silicone powder from the pumice and sand has been linked to lung disease among the workers at these processing plants. In order to protect the workers, manufacturers must invest in very costly industrial equipment (called "blasting cabinets") and/or have the workers suit up to prevent being exposed to the silicone dust. The more responsible manufacturers have been doing this for some time. (In the Appendix is a list of some manufacturers who are only working with environmentally — and humanly safe procedures. **Levi's** leads the charge. No surprises there.)

Another solution to the silicone problem is enzyme washing. Using an enzyme bath with organic enzyme-like cellulose produces the same effect as bleaching and sandblasting. The other advantage is that the fabric is less damaged and tends to last longer than the pumice-blasted fabric. Some manufacturers use a combination of enzymes and pumice to create the desired finish.

Regardless of how environmentally sensitive a manufacturer is, there are a number of chemicals used in the production of denim that are not friendly to the environment. These days most governments have put denim manufacturers' feet to the fire. As a result, the organic chemicals used in denim production, such as starch and dye, are now treated through biological methods and waste materials from production are processed in compliance with stringent regulations designed to keep toxins out of the local water supply.

Once the denim fabric has been dyed and woven, it's ready for the assembly line where the patterns for each style of jeans are cut. The actual sewing is done with each operator working on a specific part of the jeans: pockets, seams, zippers, etc. When the sewing process is done, if the material hasn't yet been treated, some manufacturers then garment-wash the finished product, using one or more of the distressing methods described above.

So, as you can see it's a very labor and raw material-intensive process. The next time you find that perfect pair of jeans, please keep in mind what went into their production and all the people down the line — from the cotton farmers to the factory workers — who helped make them available to you as a consumer.

2

Defining our Terms

*We'll take a look at the descriptions of
various jeans in terms of their style (basic cuts)
and their rise (high, medium, and low.)*

The Cut

There are seven basic cuts. (I know crops are popular now, but they're not included here. Frankly, very few women can wear them without looking proportionally odd. You have to be pretty tall and generally not Plus sized.)

1) **Skinny** jeans hug every curve, and are most often found with a mid or high rise. (Yes, they sometimes come in very low rise as well, but super low rise skinnies border on tasteless IMHO.) Super skinnies can over-emphasize ample hips or bottom; if you are slender and if you're well-endowed they can make you look top-heavy. The more weight you carry from the waist down, the denser fabric you want to look for in a skinny.

Caveat: enjoy your super skinnies, if you can wear them, but you **must** buy skinnies with at least 2% synthetics in order to be comfortable. Otherwise you'll constantly be tugging at them at the knees, crotch, calves, etc. And then there's this little issue: there are stories, rare but no joke, of women passing out because their jeans have cut off their circulation at the femoral artery! In my recommendations for each body type I have generally tried to include those that have at least 2% stretch fiber. But always go by your own comfort level. Fashion should never be a source of suffering.

2) Slim or Straight jeans are straight from the hip to the ankle
and are usually not tapered. These types of narrow jeans used to
be called "cigarette" or "stovepipe." They come in all rises, but a
mid- to high rises will visually lengthen your legs. **Ankle** jeans
— those that end above or at the ankle -are tapered in at the hem.
Straight jeans can make short legs appear longer and developed
thighs appear more slender, particularly if, as with skinnies, you
opt for a darker rinse, a denser fabric, and a higher percentage of
stretch material. As with flares, they can tend to be a little tight
around the knee, particularly for those who are somewhat
muscular.

3) Bootcuts are slightly looser through the thighs than slim or
straight jeans and have a graceful widening from knee to hem.
They're found in all rises: high, medium, and low and are
flattering to just about every body shape.

4) Flares are kind of retro style, similar to bootcut but
are more fitted from the thigh to the knee and flare out
to a much wider circumference at the hem. They are
intended to just skim the floor and give only the tiniest
peak of your shoes. These work best on taller, slender
bodies, or those with wider shoulders than hips.

5) Boyfriend jeans are what they imply.
Think about how jeans often fit on a male:
loose at every point of contact with the body,
and usually mid or low rise. (Typically, men's
waists are the same size as or larger than their
hips, hence, no need for high rises or fitted
waists.) They work for many bodies but
someone with shorter legs or a pronounced
middle can look a little sloppy in them unless
they're a little more closely fitting or worn
with heels or boots. The latest iteration of this style, the **"Girlfriend"**
jean, is essentially a boyfriend jean with slimmer legs. One option is to
simply go one or two sizes down in a boyfriend jean if you still want the

relaxed look but want something a little sexier. And to look more relaxed or create the illusion of more volume to your legs you can always go one size up.

6) Relaxed jeans or sometimes called **"Natural Fit"** are more fitted than "Boyfriend" in the seat and thighs and rest at your natural waist (meaning they have a higher rise.) They're sometimes tapered at the ankle. They can work for a variety of body shapes unless you're very wide in the hips, in which case they can make you look shapeless or even exaggerate your hips. But a heads up: some can veer dangerously close to "Mom jeans." You just don't want to go there…even if some manufacturers these days are touting them as the new and latest "thing.")

7) Trouser jeans are a kind of misnomer, as often they are much more tailored than traditional jeans and function pretty much like, well trousers. Still, I'm going to include them here because they are a very popular style and cover a multitude of sins for many body types. They tend to have a higher waist, a wider waistband, and lack a yoke, the triangular piece of fabric below the waist band and above the derrière in traditional jeans. (See "Yoke" in the following section.) Think of trouser jeans simply as a less exaggerated bootcut with fewer jeans features: stitching, rivets, and patch pockets. They often have horizontal or "welt" pockets. Because they skim past the hips and bottom they are very flattering to body shapes that tend to carry their weight below the waist. (To be perfectly honest, you won't see many recommendations for trouser jeans here because it was hard to find them. Maybe they'll be more popular soon.)

I also need to address the elephant in the room: "jeggings." Quite frankly, I love them. And if you own a pair you know why: they are profoundly comfortable. And they tend to suit many body shapes, likely because of the high amount of polyester and Spandex in them. But they encompass such an enormous category unto themselves that I just didn't include them here. And, they don't always translate as sophisticated in the way that a well-cut pair of jeans might, not to mention they stretch out of shape more quickly than traditional jeans. So don't give me grief for not including them. Just wear them and enjoy them — as I do.

Finally, some adventurous manufacturers these days have even designed Palazzo style jeans, wide-leg culottes in denim, and more recently you'll see something more like the bellbottoms that were common in the 1960s. But frankly, these don't express the spirit and intent of what jeans were created for. They're more like denim used as fashion, which can also be extremely hip and sophisticated.

The Rise

There are three basic rises:

1) **High rise**, meaning the waistline sits approximately at or only slightly below your own natural waistline. Higher rise jeans can elongate the look of the leg if your own rise (distance from waist to crotch) is short. If you have a long rise and a short waist (distance from bottom of bust to natural waistline) they can make your torso look even shorter. Those looking for tummy control would do well to look for any jeans with a higher rise.

2) **Mid rise**, meaning an inch or two below your own waistline. Mid rises are the most universally flattering and found an all styles of jeans.

3) **Low rise**, meaning just above street legal (unlike the ultra-low rise, fashionable a few years back, that was IMHO *below* street legal), works for someone with a shapely bottom and/or fairly slim tummy. You'll mostly see them in boyfriend, skinny, and bootcut jeans.

The Details

Now let's look at the details of jeans construction. These will help you understand why specific jeans work for different bodies. To be perfectly honest, if you just remember these guidelines you'll likely the able to pick out the right pair on your own, without even looking at my recommendations — which is a good thing since manufacturers change styles so fast that if you find a pair you like it's a good bet they'll be discontinued next season. That's one of the reasons I recommend buying multiples of something you like, particularly when it's a classic style.

So here are the details you want to keep in mind.

Embellishments Bling-y additions such as bedazzling and other "gems" along the sides and bottom (honestly, how does one sit comfortably in those?) changes ordinary jeans from a traditionally Natural style to something more Dramatic or Romantic in style essence. Embroidery and patchwork additions read as Youthful. So unless you have a lot of Drama, Romance, or Youthful in your personal fashion style you may want to stick with fewer embellishments. Also, always keep in mind that embellishments draw the eye to that part of the body where they're located. Lots of embellishments are not a good idea if you're trying to camouflage or deflect attention from a particular part of your body.

Fabric The long-term wear-ability and look of a pair of jeans is very much determined by the fabric from which they are made. As described earlier, jeans are a combination of heavy twill cotton plus some stretch fiber, typically Lycra© or Spandex©. These days we're also seeing a lot of rayon and polyester in the mix, two fibers that tend to add longevity to a weave. Lycra interwoven with cotton has more tensile strength than does Spandex, although Spandex is extremely popular in the more affordable brands.

Generally, anything over 3% stretch fibers will lose its shape more quickly, particularly if you put your jeans in the dryer. Anything less than that and the cotton twill fibers will wear out more quickly over time with multiple laundering. The denser or thicker the fabric, the more it will hold you in, control bulges and create a slimmer line. Many manufacturers are now adding as much as 50% synthetics (i.e. polyester or rayon) to their blends to achieve that goal. For the purists looking for 100% cotton, you're pretty much stuck with boyfriend jeans. Cotton stretches out, which is a feature that only suits boyfriend jeans and looks sloppy pretty quickly in any other style.

Feathering, fading, and ripping Feathering is the term that describes how some areas on jeans are dyed a lighter color to mimic crease lines that would appear over time. Feathering is appropriate only on more casual jeans. Fading on the front of the thigh area or derrière will emphasize and make areas of your body look larger than they actually are which is useful if you have a disappearing bottom and very thin thighs. A kind of ombre dye — darker on the outside seams and lighter over the thighs and lower leg — adds some heft to thighs and legs, which is a valuable feature if you have very thin legs.

Rips in the knees, thighs, etc. also give the appearance of long time use and call the attention to those areas. These sometimes look a little odd unless, for example, you do a lot of physical labor or are an artist, bending down and climbing ladders to work on giant canvasses in your studio — and would therefore likely *have* rips in your jeans! In this book I avoided including a lot of ripped jeans because it's likely that within a year or two they will be out of style. Or, your own will already have authentic rips. Of course, your naturally ripped, long-loved jeans will never be out of style!

Hems and cuffs Straight leg or skinny jeans that come to the ankle and cuffed jeans that hit a few inches above the ankle will visually shorten your legs. If you are petite (and particularly if your legs are short or muscular in proportion to your torso) you might want to just avoid cuffed or ankle jeans unless you are wearing them with heels, boots or neutral color flats that elongate the look of your leg. If you're particularly long legged, cuffs can bring a nice balance to your proportions. The bigger the cuff, the shorter your leg will look.

Inseam This one's the no-brainer: the distance from crotch to hem line. The longer your legs, the longer will be this measurement. In straight leg jeans an inseam that is too long for you is not going to make a difference in the overall line or shape of the jeans. You can always get them hemmed or turn up the cuff. In boot-cut jeans you'll want to make sure that, if you have to hem them, the widest part continues gracefully and proportionally to the rest of your leg.

For you DIY ladies, here's a link to **hemming your own jeans**.

Outer seam Some jeans have an outer seam that is placed slightly forward from the actual side line of your leg. The advantage of these is that they tend to make your thighs look slimmer.

Pockets The size, placement, and embellishments of pockets will make your derrière look larger, smaller, more elevated, lower, or saggy.

Size If you have an ample bottom, look for somewhat larger pockets.
Small pockets will only make your bum look ginormous in comparison. If
you have a small bottom, you can go with mid-size or larger pockets as
long as they don't end at or below your butt crease, in which case they
will make your bottom disappear.

Placement Higher set pockets will give a sagging derrière — or any
derrière for that matter — some "lift." Pockets set wide apart make your
hips/bottom look wider. Pockets that are centered over your bum or set
close together will make your bottom look smaller. Pockets — especially
large ones — that end at the crease where your derrière meets your leg
will visually drag your butt down. (Frankly, I don't understand why they
even make those on women's jeans.) Side seam pockets that are deeply
angled or rounded can make hips look bigger, particularly when you sit or
bend down. Horizontal slit — or "welt" — pockets above the hip bone,
particularly those that are set high on the front and/or back of the jeans
will lie flat and make your hips look narrower.

Embellishments as discussed above if your bottom is ample (or if you
consider it overly ample) you might want to avoid pocket embellishments
— obvious stitching, bling, feathering, etc. Pockets with embellishment
can add the illusion of volume and shape to a shapeless bottom. Logo or
trademark stitching with rounder shapes creates visual curves. Stitching in
the same color as the jeans deemphasizes a derriere.

Shape Square-ish pockets — particularly large ones — visually flatten
your bottom unless the bottom of the pocket has a triangular shape
pointing downward. Pockets with rounded bottoms make your derriere
look rounder. If you have a flat bottom, you can create the illusion of a
rounder one with flap pockets.

Rinse This describes the color of the denim fabric, ranging from a very
light powdery blue to nearly black. The lighter the color, the larger will be
the appearance of your legs, bottom, and thighs. The darker the color the
more streamlined and lengthened will be the appearance of your legs,
bottom, and thighs. Lighter rinses shorten you; darker rinses lengthen you.
Darker indigo is more formal and sophisticated; lighter blues or brighter
colors are more casual. For some reason you'll find that with many
manufacturers the color of the rinse dramatically changes the size of the
jeans. (Read the customer reviews carefully to determine if you need to go

up or down a size.)

FYI: the color of some indigo dyes used in denim is somewhat unflattering to those whose color palette leans more to the Warm/Rich autumnal category. (Learn more in Chapter 1 of my book Shopping for the Real You: Know Your Colors.) But jeans have become so universal that they are now considered a classic. So, everyone can wear them regardless of their individual coloring. Also, because they're worn on the bottom half of the body their color doesn't cast an unflattering reflection on the face. They will translate as a neutral, particularly in the darker rinses. For those with warmer color palettes, darker washes work best.

Rise The distance from the waistband to the crotch. The front rise (starting at the middle point of the front of the waistband) will usually be lower than the back rise (from the back middle point of the waistband.) The difference between the front and the back rise is called the "pitch." The curvier and more elevated your behind, the greater the pitch should be in order to fit your waist and bottom well. The smaller the pitch, the more likely you'll end up with "plumber's crack" when you sit down — particularly if you have an ample behind. If you have a fairly flat bottom you can often go with a lower rise both in the front and the back. If your hips are small or are similar in size to your waist you won't need an extreme pitch.

The relationship between the length of your torso (measuring from the bottom of your bust line to your navel) your front rise, and your legs will determine whether you look better in high rise or low rise jeans. Most people look good in a mid-rise. If you have a long torso (or what is called a "long waist") you can wear higher rise jeans. If you have a short torso you'll look better in a rise that sits a little below your natural waistline and has a higher rise in the back. If you have a short rise and a short waist don't even think about high-rise jeans. They will totally eclipse your waist. Regardless of your torso length, if your legs are short you'll look leggier in a mid-or slightly lower rise and fairly straight or bootcut jeans.

Waistband Often, if you find the right fit for your derrière the next challenge is getting a waistband that fits. If you have curves, look for jeans with a contoured waistband. You don't want to spend a fortune at the tailors constantly taking in the waistband for all your jeans. The greater the difference between your hip measurement and your waist the more likely you'll find your best fit in "curvy" styles specifically designed to accommodate that difference.

Yoke This is the triangular piece of fabric in the back of the jeans just below the bottom of the waistband and above the top of the pocket. Not all jeans have a yoke (trouser jeans do not) but the curvier your derrière and the more highly placed it is the more important is that piece of fabric. It's what hugs and defines your curves. A rounded yoke creates the illusion of a rounder bottom. The deeper the center point of the yoke the more it hugs those cheeks. An inverse yoke, one that starts high at the mid-point of your backside and curves down on either side of your cheeks, will flatter a rounder bottom. A small or flattish bum can benefit from a more steeply angled yoke or even a reversed yoke. (I've only found one manufacturer that does this but it certainly looks like it will work: Salsa.) The shallower the angle of the yoke the more the pant leg will fall straight down from the hip with no emphasis on your bottom (and beware "plumber's crack" in these kinds of jeans.) A completely horizontal yoke will make your hips and waist look wide and about the same size. That works for boyfriend jeans and women with the Flute shaped body and hips, but if you want to create or emphasize curves, you need an angled or curved yoke.

Note: the deeper the entire yoke (horizontally), the lower the pockets will have to be. So if you want to de-emphasize a sagging bum, look for a yoke that is narrower near the hip line, so that the pockets sit higher.

The Perfect Fit

Before we delve into the details of the right jeans for your body type it's good to think about these questions.

How important is comfort? I'll answer that one for you: it should be your #1 consideration. If they're not comfortable, if they pull in the wrong way, if they show what you don't want to show or emphasize what you don't want emphasized or make your proportions look funny you're not going to wear them. Don't waste your money, no matter how cute they are on the mannequin, the movie star, or anyone else.

Where will you wear them? Do you need a pair for dressy events like date night or will they be strictly for casual dressing? Are they a work staple? Are you looking for something trendy — like ripped jeans — or more classic like a dark rinse bootcut? Or do you just want something to knock around the house in? My wardrobe consultant, Hella Tsaconas always asks her clients: "Where are you going and what do you want to communicate?"

What's your price point? Has experience shown you that a pair of Levi's under 60 bucks will serve you just fine, or do you really want something more high-end? (In the body shape sections, I've list several pair at each price point — high, mid and low.)

Okay, now you're ready to find the perfect pair of jeans.

As with all clothes shopping it starts with understanding your **body type**. In my book ***Shopping for the Real You***, I described what is commonly considered to be the five basic body types: Flute, Apple, Hourglass, Pear and Triangle (or what often is now called "Strawberry.") For an overall wardrobe those five categories serve the purpose of identifying most of us pretty well most of the time.

But when it comes to buying jeans we need to get very specific. Finding the right fit is a lot like buying a bra. Just as two women with the same measurements can't always wear the exact same bra, two so-called **"Apple"** shaped bodies won't necessarily be able to wear the same jeans. And, regardless of body shape, we're not all the same height nor do we have the same level of muscle tone. So, in the same way that we are each a combination of unique color and style types, (something I go into great detail about in my *Shopping* book) many of us are also a combination of body shapes.

For example, somebody who is a **"Flute"** shape but is a little bit flabby around the middle may want to look at the recommendations for the **"Apple"** shaped body. Or, someone who has **"Hourglass"** proportions but tends to gain weight in their bottom and thighs may also want to look at the recommendations for the **"Pear"** shaped body. (You might find the same jeans recommended for both the "Pear" shape and the "Hourglass" body.) **"Strawberries"** on the thin side might find that some recommendations for the **"Flute"** body can actually work very well for them. And the heavier ones may want to look in the **"Apple"** recommendations. Because there are many variations on the Flute shape body (tall, short, muscular, long torso, short torso) I've included more recommendations for this body type than the others.

If you're not exactly sure which body shape you have, just think about where you tend to hold excess weight over time. Most of us are pretty much straight up and down until puberty. Also, our bodies tend to change after childbirth and/or menopause. Pay attention to the areas where you need more or less room in your jeans, combine that with an understanding of how the proportions of your upper body relate to those of your lower body, and let those be your guide.

As previously described in the "Detail" section, getting the right fit means paying attention to some pretty intimate details: the shape, elevation, and size of your bottom; the size and shape of your tummy; the proportional relationship between your hips and your waist; the length of your legs and their shape; the size of your thighs. Whew! If any one of those — or all of them — cause you pain or consternation, cheer up! There is a pair of jeans for every derrière, leg length, tummy, etc.

There is another very important consideration (two, in fact) for picking the right pair of jeans. These were so important that I included an entire chapter about them in *Shopping for the Real You*. They are: Balance and Proportion. To appear balanced and in proportion you need to pay attention to how the top half of your body relates to the bottom half. (If you're tall, petite or plus sized proportions become extremely important.)

For that reason, at the end of the recommendations section are suggestions for how to style your jeans for each body shape. These include things such as what tops, jackets, and accessories are flattering with the jeans that work for that body shape.

Where's the best place to shop for jeans?

I'm not going to tell you that you shouldn't shop online. (Every one of the recommendations here is linked to an online retailer.) You can get some pretty amazing deals online, especially when the site is having a sale. But everyone knows that online shopping is hit or miss. You really have to try something on to know if it will fit. So, to avoid paying a lot for returns keep an eye out for free shipping deals and coupons. Most sites offer discounts and coupons fairly frequently, especially if you're on their mailing lists. Once you get on that list you'll become their new best friend. Expect to receive special offers every week.

Whenever — and wherever — you try on jeans give them a good workout: sit down, cross and uncross your legs, bend over, squat, (and look for any rear end exposure) tuck in your top or tee, let it out, put on an outerwear piece, swap out different shoe heights. Then check to see if there's any sagging in the bottom or knees. Check to see if they ride up on your legs or are very tight around the knees and require some tugging and pulling to get them to relax back down.

A lot of skinny jeans do stretch out (and that's not a terrible thing – you don't want to be encased in your clothes) so keep that in mind when purchasing; you may need to go a size down.

Most manufacturers switch up styles fairly quickly. If you find something that appeals to you, you may not want to wait too long to see if it will go on sale. It might be sold out in your size. If you love it and it's a classic you may want to buy an extra pair. (Wish I had bought an extra pair of those NYDJ trouser jeans I found five years ago…) A particular style that you'll find online may not be available at a department or specialty store. The reverse is also true: some jeans are distributed solely through large retailers.

The differences between two styles from the same manufacturer (in fabric, cut and even the rinse) can be significant. In a slim jean you might have to go one size up and in a boyfriend or relaxed jean, one size down. And a number of manufacturers are purposely sizing their jeans smaller than your normal size (NYDJ is notorious for this) to make you feel slimmer. Read customer reviews carefully and look at the details of each pair; pocket placement size, rise, inseam, etc.

Your Body Type Recommendations

In each of the body type sections below I've indicated the unique challenges presented for that body and then offer suggestions for the types of styles that work best for that body. Following that are some of my specific recommendations at every price point. (Full disclosure: some of them are from affiliates I work with and I receive a small fee if you order something.) These recommendations are for jeans that I personally tried on and discovered where they do and don't fit me — ergo, which bodies they *would* fit — or were suggested by my readers, or were the result of my lengthy research.

Many of those listed are available in multiple color rinses in addition to the one shown in the link. Considering that just about every fashion house and department store carries women's jeans, I couldn't possibly include all of them. So I tried to limit the list to those that were most readily available.

You'll notice that there might be multiple recommendations from the same manufacturer for a specific body type. That's because some manufacturers make jeans that tend to work for that body type. I also didn't include anything overly trendy or extreme. You'll also see that most of the recommendations are for lower-to-middle priced styles because, really, how many of you are going to shell out $300 for a pair of jeans? OK – yes, some of the high end are kind of cool, but you can often get "cool" for less. I've added notations after the prices to indicate if the style is available in extended sizes (**P** = petite; **PL** = plus; **T** = tall.) Occasionally the link provided for a specific pair might take you to only one variation (tall, e.g.) but elsewhere on the site will be the petite or plus version.

I can guarantee one thing: by the time you read this many of these recommended styles will be on sale at HUGE discounts from the prices I've shown. If the specific style listed is no longer available, the same manufacturer will very likely have something similar in current stock that will work for you.

At the end of this book you'll find an Resource List of manufacturers, including details about what kinds of bodies they cater to and which ones offer extended sizes. Plus sizes is considered to be size 16 (US) and up. Several of the jeans I've recommended are available up to size 24, but it is a challenge to find a lot of size variety from the higher end manufacturers who, let's face it, cater to a fairly exclusive and often skinny crowd. For tall ladies I looked for inseams of at least 34" and higher.

Finally, if you already have a pair of jeans that you love and just want to find something similar, take your beloved jeans with you when you shop, or get out a tape measure and measure the inseam, the rises (both front and back) the waist, and the hips. Then take the jeans — or your measurements — with you. A good sales associate should be able to find a new pair that match. And if you're obsessive about a pair you've owned for a while, check out the "Bespoke" section in the Resource List to see if you can have them duplicated somewhere.

OK — now you're ready to look at some jeans for your body type. Remember, you may be able to wear styles that work for more than one shape. For example, many of the jeans that work for a pear shaped body can also work for an hourglass shaped body. So, look at the illustrations in Chapter 5, "How to Style Your Jeans." That might give you some clues as to which ones you can wear.

Your Personal Jeans Profile

Because jeans are designed for the lower half of the body the recommendations here are, of course, primarily related to how they fit your lower half. But as we learned in the previous chapter, proportion is equally important, i.e. if you're top-heavy you want to avoid super skinnies; if you're very muscular you want less fading or bling around your thighs; if you have a flat derrière you don't want large low hanging pockets, etc. In the next chapter are descriptions and illustrations for specific silhouettes to wear with your jeans in order to create the most pleasing visual relationship between your upper and lower body.

For most of you the recommendations for your body type will be fairly consistent regardless of your height, weight, and proportions. But at the end of the body type descriptions are additional suggestions that address variations within each body type. Also, I always recommend looking at online customer reviews to find out about things such as whether you need to go up or down a size.

Apple Shape — Juicy and Leggy

You apples have gotten a bad rap (or sometimes give yourselves a bad rap) and I'm here to set the record straight. You ladies often have great cleavage, long legs and slender ankles. What's not to love? Now, there are Apples and then there are "Apples." Over time that little bit extra you tend to carry around your middle can start to take up more real estate in the upper half of your body: arms, breasts, and back. So you're going to want to pay attention to how you style your jeans, i.e. what to wear on the top of your body (see illustrations in the next chapter.) And of course, you want to make sure that your jeans aren't creating a shelf for your tummy to hang over or love handles to sit on, or have a rise that is so high that your tummy pooches out underneath it. Fortunately there are a lot of options that will flatter your lovely body.

> **Your challenge:** keeping your waist in check and emphasizing your legs.

> **What works:** Actually, you lucky apples can wear many different styles of jeans. In fact, don't be afraid of straight or tapered straight leg jeans. Jeans with fading over the thighs or some kind of embellishments or rips put the attention on your long legs. When buying skinnies, you might want to go one size up.

> A Mid rise straight or bootcut in a dark wash can be your regular go-to. You can also do a relaxed straight leg jean. The ones with tummy control are an added boon (Jag, Salsa, e.g.). Trouser jeans emphasize the length of your legs, help keep your tummy in place, and balance out your midsection. And guess what? You can even likely do flares, assuming you are an average size or taller "apple."

> In general, the darker washes tend to lengthen and narrow the look of your midsection. Rear flap pockets or cute pocket embellishments-and you tend to like playful things-will draw attention to and emphasize your bottom, rather than your belly. (Hudson and Miss Me have several.) You're going to want pockets of an average size and spaced high and wider apart. If you

can find rounded rather than angled pockets or pocket stitching, those will help to give the appearance of a rounder shape to your bottom.

As for fabric, look for a denser weave with, preferably, at least 2% stretch fibers to help control your middle section. Avoid a significant "pitch" or curved waistband. You don't want to create a shelf for your tummy.

Avoid: You probably want to avoid the super skinnies as they can emphasize the imbalance between your upper and lower body. Anything with too high of a rise (anything right act or above your natural waistline) is going to call attention to your wider mid-section. Very high rises can even make your waist look larger. You can wear low rises but make sure your top, blouse or sweater is long enough to cover any "overlap." Also, boyfriend jeans, unless they're slim fitting, can make shorter apples appear a little dumpy and curve-less. If you're tall you can certainly wear cuffed jeans. They'll draw attention to your lower legs and balance out your upper body.

And...

Flat-bottom Apples: Do not — repeat — do not wear loose, baggy boyfriend jeans with large, low placed pockets. Your derriere will entirely disappear. (You probably already know that.) Look for higher set, rounded pockets or those with rounded stitching or embellishments — even flap pockets.

Plus-sized Apples: If you're carrying a lot more around your middle, boyfriend jeans can look too baggy on you. Leave them on the boyfriend. Generally, a straight, tapered or bootcut is more flattering.

Petite Apples: A looser skinny can work if you're wearing heels or neutral colored ballet flats, both of which will extend the line of your leg. Straight leg or slightly bootcut styles will make you look longer and leaner and will emphasize your legs.

Short waisted apple: A slightly exaggerated pitch (higher back rise and lower front rise) will elongate your torso. It will also draw attention to your bottom and away from your waist. Just make sure you're not hanging over the front of your jeans.

Tall Apples: You can go with a higher rise since you have longer legs but you probably don't want to any higher than slightly below your natural waist. If you're disproportionately short-waisted, a lower rise will bring the rest of you into balance. Skinnies are a little iffy on some tall apples (it can throw off their proportions.) You're the "Apple" that can wear boyfriend jeans pretty easily.

Try these:

Low End:

American Eagle "Kick" Bootcut $40-50 P, T
GAP Straight Jeans $80-90 P, PL
L.L. Bean True Shape Slim Leg $60 P, PL, T
Lee Modern Midrise Fit Dream Skinny $28 P, T, PL
Levi's 414 Classic Straight Jeans $54 P, T
Levi's Classic Bootcut $54 P, PL, T
Macy's Style & Co Straight Leg $49 P, PL, T
Old Navy Curvy Bootcut $30 P, PL, T
Walmart Faded Glory $13-26 P PL
Wrangler "Aura" $30-$59 P, PL, T

Middle End:

Calvin Klein Straight Leg $59-$69 P
Chico's So Slimming Girlfriend Jeans $99 PL
Eddie Bauer "Slightly Curvy $80-$90 P, PL, T
LEL Curvy Bootcut $79 PL, T
Lucky Brand Skinny Mid Rise $100
Lucky Mid rise Bootcut $100 T
Macy's INC Boyfriend $70-$100
Mavi Bootcut $98 T
Miss Me Bootcut $99 T
NYDJ "Barbara" Bootcut $114-$134 P, T, PL
NYDJ "Billie" Mini Bootcut $114-$144 P, PL
NYDJ "Marilyn" Straight Leg $109-$134 P, PL, T
Talbot's Straight Leg $95-100 P, PL, T

High End:

AG Skinny $173-$225 T
James Jeans Straight Hunter $185 PL only
Joe's Jeans Ankle $178-198
Joe's Jeans Bootcut $158-$198
MIH Daily $240
Paige High Rise $159- $229-$189 P, T
Seven for All Mankind Dojo $159-$199 P
True Religion Becca Bootcut $179 T

Flute Shape — Rockin' the Runways

Okay — you likely already know you can wear almost any cut of jeans. Yours is the body shape of many models. So, generally, most of you (OK — maybe not petites) don't have to work hard to get a long and lean appearance. If anything you want jeans that suggest a little bit of curve to the waist, hips and derriere. Also, you lucky **Flutes** tend to gain weight equally throughout your body, so you're unlikely to have a disproportionate "spread" in your waist, fanny, or hips over time.

However, flutes have the greatest number of variations within their category, (which is why you will see more jeans recommendations in this category than in the others.) Those variations are based on how buff you are and whether or not you have some cleavage and/or derriere. Those elements come into play when considering proportional balance between the upper and lower halves of your body. So pay particular attention to the keys after each recommendation (P, PL, T) to see whether the particular jeans you see are available for petites, tall or plus sizes. And look at the comments below addressed to those of you flutes with specific challenges (long torso, muscular legs, etc.)

Your challenge: Creating a waistline and curves.

What works: Straight, skinny, bootcut, flare, you name it. You can wear them all. You can also wear boyfriend jeans with rolled cuffs. And although I agree with Tim Gunn (whom I adore) that nobody looks great in crops, most flutes can, in fact, wear cropped jeans as long as both ends of their body (upper body and feet) are anchored with more visual "weight."

Generally, a mid-to lower rise works best for you, although tall thin Flutes have one of the few bodies that can wear almost any kind of rise. And unless you have a fair amount of bootie, avoid an extreme "pitch" between the front and back rises.

If you like embellishments, you're in luck. Flutes can go with pretty much any kind of embellishment: fading, feathering, embroidery, sparkles, and rips. And high or wider set flap pockets, or any kind of embroidery or bling on your pockets will add emphasis to your bottom. Also, side seam angled or curved pockets help imply wider hips. You can also wear lighter color washes. Lucky you!

What to avoid: If you're very thin, avoid the super skinny body hugging styles, particularly if you have a flat butt; they can make you look slightly emaciated.

And...

Ample bosom: It's particularly important for buxom Flutes to look for jeans that add some oomph to their hips and bottom so as to balance out their upper bodies. That means, look for curved or angled side pockets, and have fun with embellishments, fading, rips, flap pockets etc. (Be sure to check out styling tips in chapter 5.)

Long torso: High rise jeans in both flares and bootcuts will balance out your torso and emphasize whatever amount of curve you have in your bottom or hips.

Petite: If your legs are on the short side, make sure any boyfriend jeans are cut fairly slim or go down a size. If you like rolled cuffs, wearing them with some kind of heel will elongate your legs. Everything else is fair game, except anything that ends mid-calf.

Muscular legs: Athletic flutes may want to avoid lighter colored jeans or ones with fading over the thighs. That fading — intentional or eventual (with multiple washings and wear) — will make your thighs look larger. Darker, mid-rise bootcuts and flares are your best bet. And, you can certainly wear straight or boyfriend jeans. Skinnies? Depends on just how buff you are (although Serena Williams does them spendidly!) Look for a denser fabric with a minimum of 2% spandex or Lycra, both of which will help slenderize muscular thighs. Anything too loose can make you look shorter or a little stocky. Trouser jeans are a great option for you because they give you a waistline and make your legs look lean and long.

Short waist: Best to opt for those styles that visually elongate your torso and your legs. That means you to want to avoid high rise jeans. Mid-to-lower rise, straight leg, semi skinny and, in particular, bootcut work best for you.

Try these:

Low End:

Alloy Skinny $50 PL, T
American Eagle Boyfriend $40-50 P, PL, T
American Eagle Kick Boot $45 P, PL, T
ASOS Tall Ridley High Waist Ultra Skinny $54 T GB only
Calvin Klein Ultimate Skinny $28-$54
Gap Perfect Midrise Bootcut Jeans $70 P, PL, T
Guess High Rise Skinny $44
Macy's INC 5-Pocket Skinny $35-$70
Lee's Classic Fit Monroe Straight Leg P, T $25-$30
Levi's Super Skinny $54-$98 T P, T
Old Navy Original Bootcut $30 P, PL, T
Uniqlo Ultra Stretch Jeans $40

Mid Range:

Calvin Klein Straight $70-$90
GAP High Rise Slim Straight $70
J. Crew Slim Boyfriend $110-$128 P, T,
Levi's Slim Fit $60-$90 T
Lucky Brand Skinny $80-140
Mavi "Emma" Boyfriend $98
NYDJ "Barbara" Bootcut $110 P, PL, T
NYDJ "Ami" Skinny $129-$144 P, PL
Pilcro Skinny Ankle $118-$158 P, T

High End:

AG Bootcut $178-$225, $205
AG Cigarette "Stilt" $168-$188
Diesel "Skinzee" $178-$228
7 for All Mankind Bootcut $179-$199
Hudson "Zooey" High Rise Straight $225
Hudson "Drew" Bootcut" $195-$235
J Brand "Hipster" Lowrise $228
Paige "Verdugo" Ultra Skinnies $169-$299

Hourglass: putting the "X" in sexy

Broader shoulders, narrow waist and broader hips: va va voom! This is the body shape that is very forgiving even if you've added a few pounds here and there over time. They just emphasize all your curves. But you'll often find that a pair of jeans that is flattering for your hips and backside is too wide for your waist. Many hourglasses have to accept the trade-off for having a sexy body: having a good tailor. I've tried to list as many recommendations as possible that will help you avoid having to have them altered, but the reality is that often you will have to have the waist adjusted.

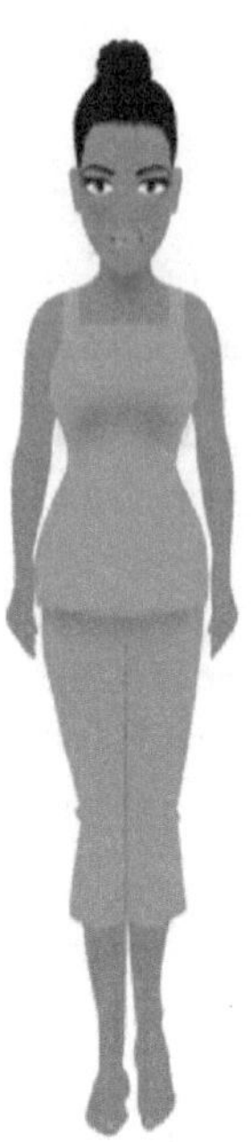

Now, in case you've been hiding under a rock, you know that "booty" is in! So I'm not going to tell you extremely ample bottomed Hourglasses to not wear skinnies. It's your call. Just know that the "flaunt your booty" look is for extremely young women, particularly those in the entertainment industry. And as I mentioned earlier, you definitely don't want to go with any super tight skinny fit that might cut off your circulation anywhere! The listed recommendations here are primarily for ladies who want to dress up without being known just for their derrières.

The good news: there are a lot of options for you in the low to mid-price range. The not so good news, if you like premium denim, you just have fewer options, particularly for plus size and petites. (**Paige Denim** just announced that they're going to be offering "curvy" styles soon, but unfortunately not in time for this edition.) So I've included a number of styles that are also listed in the Pear Shaped body section, as these often will fit an hourglass body as well.

> **Your challenge:** Getting the pitch (difference between the back and front rise) right, keeping proportional balance.

> **What works:** Look for styles that elongate your legs, as the overall line of an hourglass body is broken up by your proportionally smaller waist, which sometimes can make you look a little bit shorter than you actually are (with the exception of course, of tall hourglasses.) If you're somewhat longer-waisted a high rise can work for you and emphasize your waist. In fact, for many of the premium denim manufacturers, the only styles that will fit your waist without gapping at the back are higher rises. For all hourglasses look for a contour waistband with a higher pitch in back.

Mid-rise bootcut jeans are pretty much universally flattering on all Hourglasses. Trouser jeans are always a nice option for Hourglasses if you're looking for something more formal. (I admit I couldn't find many.) Skinnies? Sure, but just know that you really make a statement in skinnies! You can also wear a boyfriend jean (Marilyn Monroe certainly did) if your hips and derrière aren't too exaggerated. If you're petite, you want to make sure you're not hiding under baggy boyfriend jeans. Keep them a little more fitted as in what they're now calling "girlfriend" jeans, i.e., they belong to you, not your boyfriend, and are still loose and funky.

Flares? Certainly. They emphasize the wide-narrow-wide silhouette of your body shape. Just don't go for too wide a flare, particularly if you're petite or a little chunky. Or at least pair them with a higher, chunky-heeled shoe. But don't be afraid of slightly body-hugging styles, as long as the waist fits. Wearing those with heels is not only sexy it lengthens you, one of the goals toward proportional balance for an Hourglass.

Fading and feathering are best if your thighs aren't overly hefty. And you can certainly go for pocket embellishments…but why? You don't really need them. Just keep them playful. Too much bling can look cheap on an hourglass.

And now, the exception to my rule about leggings: the reality is, when you have an hourglass figure it's often extremely difficult to find jeans that will fit your hips and your waist. For that reason I've included a couple of "jeggings" for the hourglass category.

Avoid: the extremes of super baggy and super skinny and anything that makes your legs or your torso appear short, (particularly if your hips are ample and legs are short) such as rolled cuffs or a too-high rise. Straight leg jeans are ok, and I've included some here, but might be a little uninspiring. Make sure you're not hiding your assets.

And...

Big booty: for you hourglass gals with a lot of "bass" there are a few manufacturers to check out first: **PZI** and **Mynt** are two. And **Miracle Body** has a couple of great ones. (See the Index.)

Plus sizes: For plus sized Hourglasses darker rinses are most flattering. (Also, be sure to check out the index at the back of this book for plus size jeans manufacturers.)

Try these:

Low End:

Calvin Klein Curvy Fit Bootcut $70
Eddie Bauer Stayshape Curvy High Rise $70-80 P, PL, T
Guess Sienna Curvy $44
Guess Cindy Power Skinny $44
INC Curvy Fit 5-Pocket $70
Lee's Modern Series Curvy Fit $45 P, PL, T
Lee's Straight Leg $44-48
Calvin Klein Curvy Skinny $70
Old Navy Curvy Bootcut $30 P, PL, T
PZI Curve Skinny $69 T
Rock & Republic Kassandra Bootcut (runs long) $88 P,T,L
Wrangler "Aura" $44-$60 PL, T (size down)

Mid End:

Bebe "Hourglass" $89-$99
CJ by Cookie Johnson "Grace" Bootcut $98
Lane Bryant Super Rise Skinny $100-$110 PLUS, T, P
Levi's Revel Bold Curve Skinny $98-$118
Long Elegant Legs Curvy Bootcut $79-$89 PL, T
Lucky "Lolita" Skinny $80-$119 PL, T
Lucky "Sophia" Midrise Skinny $99 PL
NYDJ "Barbara" Modern Bootcut $114-$134 P, PL, T
NYDJ "Marilyn" Straight Leg $109-$134 P, PL, T
NYDJ "Alina" Legging $114-$134 P, PL,T
Silver Suki Curvy $64-$89

High End:

AG Jeans "Farrah" Skinny Contour $198
Cookie Johnson Power Relaxed Boyfriend $178
DL1961 "Florence" Instasculpt $178-$208
Joe's Jeans Boyfriend Slim $178-$225
Joe's Jeans Curvy Bootcut $158-$188 P
Mother Denim Midrise Straight $ $205-$228
7 for All Mankind "Kimmie" Contour $168-179 T
True Religion "Jennie" Skinny $169-$249 PL

Pear Shape: those sassy "bass" notes

You pears are a pretty potent combination: a delicate upper body with typically long arms and a youthful bosom — plus curvy hips and bottom and slender ankles. You're positively Rubensesque! But frankly, pears have some

of the hardest time finding the right jeans. For that reason
I've listed a LOT of jeans recommendations for you.

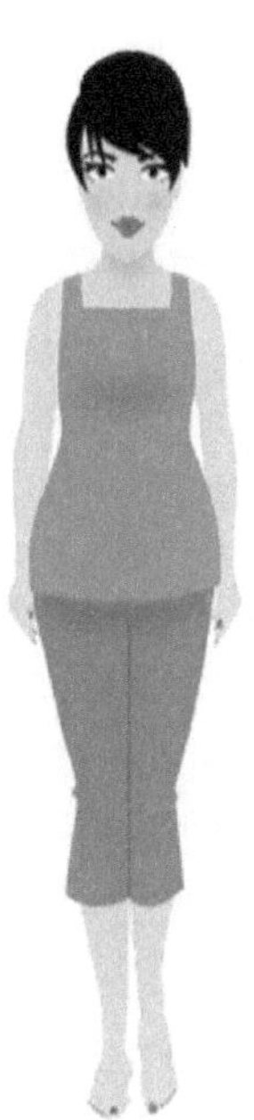

Your challenge: Your first priority is to fit your thighs
and bottom, and then to create visual balance between
your upper and lower body.

What works: Bootcut or slightly flared jeans in a darker
rinse are the most flattering options for you as they will
skim — and slim — your thighs, hold in your bottom,
and elongate your legs. Straight leg jeans are also great
on a pear-shaped body. (Make sure the inseam is long
enough to allow just a peek of your shoes.) Trousers can
work too if the rise isn't too high. Jeans with a high rise
will emphasize the disproportion between the upper and
lower half of your body. The best rise for a Pear is a
mid-rise, but you can go ever-so-slightly higher or
lower.

Also, look for a contoured waistband. (Here's where you'll find some
crossover with the recommendations for the Hourglass body.) That will
insure that your derriere is covered when you bend or stoop. Any jeans
with the outer seam slightly forward from the actual sideline of your leg
will make hips and thighs look smaller too. And, denser stretch fabrics are
your friend as they will keep your thighs in check.

Your pockets should be medium in size, definitely not small (remember
that small pockets make larger bottoms look very large in comparison)
more centered, and set higher on your bottom. That placement will give
you a nice visual "lift." So, that means just avoid very wide-set pockets.
And pocket embellishments or bling? Well, perhaps some embellishment
if you're not a very plus sized Pear. Just don't overdo it, particularly if
you're going for a more tailored look.

You can do straight leg jeans too, as long as you follow all the guidelines
for pockets, rise, and fabric. Just make sure they're straight, not tapered in
at the ankle dramatically, which will throw off your proportions.
Boyfriend jeans? Skinnies? Well, maybe boyfriend skinnies — that means
slimmer cut boyfriend jeans, and only for those more slender Pears with
longer legs. Boyfriend jeans on petite pears can often look pretty dumpy.

Proportions are crucial for you Pears. Make sure your top or jacket adds breadth to your shoulders and also ground yourself with chunkier shoes: wedges, lower thick heels, espadrilles or thick-soled sneakers. See the next chapter: "What to Wear with Your Jeans."

Avoid: With the exceptions mentioned above super skinnies and their opposites — extremely loose or very wide-leg jeans — are just plain not terribly flattering on Pears. The same goes for exaggerated pocket embellishments, fading, and anything that emphasizes your thighs and derrière. If you have jeans or trousers with horizontal slit front pockets make sure they don't start anywhere near the widest part of your hips or fanny. They will visually emphasize the width of your hips. Also avoid vertical or angled side seam pockets as they tend flare out from your hip line as you walk, bend and sit.

And...

Tall Pears: You can possibly go with more straight or even somewhat skinny jeans, as long as you wear balancing shoes and tops.

Petite Pears: Skinnies? Not great, particularly if your legs are short. Everything about the bootcut is going to flatter you most. Also, wide flares will tend to shorten the look of your legs.

Plus Pears: Just repeat after me: "step away from the skinnies…" (Yes, I know they show them in Lane Bryant, but really?) Bootcuts and not-too-wide flares are cute options.

Long Waisted Pears: You're the only pears who can get away with a high waisted flare jean and still look in balance (the Citizens for Humanity "Fleetwood" is included here just for you!)

Short waisted Pears: A slightly lower front rise and contoured waistband is essential. Forget about jeans with any waist higher than your hip line — especially straight leg jeans. They'll just read "mom jeans" on you, will shorten your torso and legs and throw you out of balance.

Try these:

Low End:

Gloria Vanderbilt "Amanda" $40-$54 P, PL
As Real As Wrangler Misses Classic Fit Bootcut $32
Wrangler Aura Instantly Slimming $30-$60 P, T, PL

Lee's Curvy Bootcut $40 P, T
Lee's Modern Curvy Straight $33 P, T
Lee's Slimming Fit "Rebound" Straight $40 P, T
Levi's "Denizen" Fit $65-$70 PL
Liz Claiborne Curvy Fit Slim $48 P
New York and Company Eva Mendes "Soho" $55-$70 P, T
Old Navy Curvy Bootcut $25-28 P, PL T

Middle End:

CJ by Cookie Johnson "Grace" Bootcut $98
Eddie Bauer Curvy Boot and Straight $70-$100 P PL T Lin
Lucky Brand "Sofia" Midrise Skinny $99 PL, T
Lucky Brand "Lolita"Bootcut $99 PL, T
Lucky Brand "Sienna" Boyfriend $80-119 PL
NYDJ Boyfriend $124-$134 P, PL
NYDJ Slim Ankle Jeans $109-148 P, PL, T
NYDJ "Marilyn" Straight Leg $109-$134 P, PL, T
Ralph Lauren "Super Stretch Curvy" $90
7 Seven Hi Rise Skinny $74

High End:

7 for All Mankind "Kimmie" Contour $168-179 T
AG Jeans "Farrah" Skinny Contour $198
DL1961 "Florence" Instasculpt $178-$208
Joe's Jeans Curvy Bootcut" $179
Paige "Lou Lou" Flare $179-$199 P, T
Paige Verdugo Ankle $199-$229 P
Paige Jimmy Jimmy Slim Boyfriend $199

Juicy Strawberry: Oh So Huggable

The Strawberry is often typically described as a triangle-shaped body. That means you are structurally broad through the shoulders and narrow in the waist and hips, often with slender legs. Many Strawberries also tend to have some significant cleavage (lucky you!)

However, there are some basic differences between the typical Strawberry and thinner or more muscular triangles. Triangles, or what are often called inverted triangles, are usually flutes with broad shoulders. For thinner Triangles and Strawberries, many of the recommendations for bootcut and boyfriend jeans in the "Flute" body section will work well.

And, for the more ample Strawberry, who might have gained weight in her midsection, some recommendations for the Apple-Shape body will work.

The wonderfully charming thing about you Strawberries is that you appear warm and approachable because you have more arms and upper body to embrace. For all Strawberries, from slender to plus sized, shopping for jeans is all about creating balance and proportion.

Your challenge: Bringing balance between your upper and lower body and (if needed) adding some shape to your hips and bottom, particularly if your bottom is flatter rather than rounded.

What works: Boot-cut jeans are your best bet, as they create a nice visual symmetry of broad-narrow-broad shape from your shoulders to waist to legs. But the currently fashionable flares, wide leg jeans and even sailor-type jeans that flare out from the hip line rather than the knee, serve a similar purpose. Trouser jeans are also a nice option when you want to look more pulled together. And yes you can wear boyfriend jeans, especially with cuffs, as they draw the eye visually to your lower leg. Just don't go for anything too saggy overall, particularly in the seat. You want to emphasize your bum, not make it disappear. Slightly relaxed straight leg jeans can work for some of you too.

Generally a mid-rise is the best for your body type. Many Strawberries, particularly heavier ones, would do well to avoid higher rises as they draw the eye away from the legs, which you want to emphasize. The exception is for tall Strawberries since many flare, sailor, or bootcut jeans do, in fact, have higher rises.

Most of you, particularly those with flatter bottoms, can have a lot of fun with pocket embellishments, contrast stitching, flap pockets and bling. You also don't have to be aware of fading on thighs or derrières. Look for rounded or side angled pockets, particularly with embellishments, all of which will add visual width to a proportionally smaller hip line. Just make sure that the pockets are sized proportionately to your actual derrière.

Very large patch pockets, particularly on boyfriend jeans or on a small derrière, will simply minimize the size of your bottom.

Ample bosom: You can balance out an ample bosom with a bootcut, flare or boyfriend jean in almost any rise. Straight jeans (not super skinnies) might do the same, particularly if, like boyfriend jeans, they're rolled up and cuffed at the ankle. Both styles will bring visual harmony to a body that, especially with weight gain, might appear top-heavy.

Petites: Don't go too wide with flare or sailor type jeans.

Plus: If your weight is primarily in your upper body avoid skinnies at all cost. If you're also carrying some weight in your bottom check out some of the "Bootylicious" styles in the index.

Tall: For taller, thinner triangles and strawberries wider belts and substantial belt buckles will emphasize your waist or the middle of your torso.

Avoid: Tight skinnies, very narrow straight leg jeans, or anything tapered down to the ankle. All of them will simply emphasize the proportional narrowness of your lower body and make you look top-heavy (regardless of your bust size.)

Try these:

Low end:

American Eagle Artist Flared Jeans $50-$60 P, PL, T Link
American Eagle Favorite Boyfriend Jeans $40-$50 P, P LT Lnk
American Eagle Kick Boot $40-$50 P, PL, T
GAP "Real" Straight Leg $70 P, PL, T
L.L. Bean 1912 Straight Leg P, PL, T
Lee's Easy Fit "Frenchie" Bootcut $40 P, PL, T
Lee's Modern Series "Dream" $48-$52 P, PL, T
Levi's 315 Bootcut Jeans $65 P, PL
Old Navy "Rockstar" Midrise $35-$40 P, PL, T
Wrangler Midrise Skinny $40 P, T
Wrangler Retro "Mae" $60 PL, T

Middle End:

Armani Skinny $90
Calvin Klein Boyfriend $90
Guess Midrise Skinny $89-$128 P, T

J. Crew Slim Boyfriend $125 P, PL, T
Lucky "Sweet" $80-$119 PL, T
Michael Kors "Selma" $78 $100 P
NYDJ "Billie" Mini Bootcut $114-144 P, PL
NYDJ "Teresa" Trouser $124-$134 P, PL
NYDJ "Boyfriend"/"Girlfriend" $124-$134

High End:

AG Jeans Ex Boyfriend $112-$245
True Religion "Billie" Straight $179 T
Joe's Jeans Bootcut $185-$189 P, T
Mother Denim "Tomboy" $228-$285
Paige Denim "Lou Lou" Flare $199 T
Seven for All Mankind Flare $159-$199
True Religion "Becca" Bootcut $179 T

How to Style Your Jeans

(Hint: It's all about proportion, proportion, proportion)

D ressing up a pair of jeans is one of the most fun fashion exercises. It's also one of the easiest. Jeans can take you from your kid's soccer game to date night with the simple change of a top, jacket, or pair of shoes.

For each person the key is in styling for your body type and proportions. In fact, all dressing is about proportion.

So take an objective — but loving — look at yourself paying attention to the relationship between your upper body and lower body, to the length and shape of your legs, and to your general body shape. That will help you understand what needs to be emphasized and what might need to be brought into balance.

And, by no means should you feel this will limit you significantly in what you can wear! You'll see that there are many suggestions for each body type that will work for you.

A few general rules for extended body types

Most of these guidelines are already addressed in each body type section. But repetition sometimes helps us drive home a point so that we don't forget it.

Petites: Proportional dressing means "no extremes." In general, petites tend to look more balanced and lengthened with a little more tailored look. You've already read the value of keeping your pockets on the smaller scale and the bling, fading, feathering and "distressed" look a little toned down. The same goes for tops and jackets. A petite Strawberry, for example, can wear a peplum top to emphasize her hips, but will want to make sure the flare is not exaggerated and the length works for her body.

Plus: Proportion is very important when styling jeans for plus sizes. For example, a plus size Hourglass can certainly wear a lot of the recommended figure-enhancing jackets and tops. But for certain occasions, she may want instead to go with those that are a little more tailored, a little less, well, "hourglass-y." The same goes for a plus size Pear: keep things tasteful when it comes to showing off your assets.

Tall: Taller women might want to pay particular attention to the color and pattern in their tops and jackets. Even if your coloring and personal style type can handle strong color contrast and bold patterns, these elements make a big statement on a tall woman. If you can carry it off with confidence, sure, why not make a statement? But you feel at all self-conscious take it all down a notch. Try a more tone on tone color palette or a more classic silhouette.

General Guidelines for Styling Different Kinds of Jeans

Styling different kinds of jeans depends largely on your body shape so keep in mind the recommendations for your body shape when considering these guidelines.

Bootcuts: Keep the bottom hem of your sweaters, tops or jackets between your waist and the top of your hip line. You already have a fair amount of fabric below the hip line. You don't want to get lost underneath your clothes. You can wear a longer coat or jacket as long as what's underneath is more formfitting and or defines your waist.

The advantage of bootcut jeans is that you can wear almost any kind of footwear: booties, heels, sneakers, and sandals both with and without a heel, and flats can work but are more youthful in style, and tend to get a little lost.

Boyfriend: Boyfriend jeans cry out for simplicity and tailoring in the rest of your outfit. You can wear a loose tee as long as it doesn't end below the waistband of your jeans and whatever you wear over it also ends near your natural waist. If you wear a tailored jacket or blazer or a moto jacket, the shirt, sweater or tee underneath it should end at your waist or should be tucked into your jeans.

These also require very strategic choices in footwear. You can either go natural (like a deck shoe or sneakers), tailored (like ballet flats or brogues) or sexy (like sandals or stilettos.) Pairing boyfriend jeans with flip flops or athletic shoes will throw off your proportions and draw too much attention to your feet. Ankle boots can certainly work, but make sure that the top of the boot doesn't keep skimming the hem of the cuffs.

If you go with higher heels, keep what you wear on the top of your body more body hugging, like a tailored shirt, tee or jacket.

Skinny and Straight: Keep it short and sweet: a cropped jacket, moto jacket, waist-length sweater, peplum top or a tucked-in blouse define your waist and create balanced proportions. In fact, a peplum can bring proportional balance to strawberries or triangles, add some oomph to very slender Flutes, emphasize Hourglass curves, and can even camouflage Pear-shape hips, assuming the hem of the top is long enough and your legs are long enough that the top won't make you look squished and heavy.

But you can also continue the long, lean line of skinnies with a jacket or fitted sweater that reaches to the tips of your fingers, as long as whatever you wear under it defines the waist — or you can simply belt the sweater. Booties, boots, flats or heels are generally better than elaborate sandals for skinny jeans.

Flares: Because they are not extremely tailored and they imply a kind of floating quality the rest of your outfit has to complement that. Anything ending in a bell-shaped sleeve does this. A flow-y top, a draped surplice, or a loose-weave boat neck sweater does the same plus it balances out the width of the pants hem.

Boxy cropped jackets are a nice structural counterpoint to the flares, as are pea coats that flare slightly at the hem, or for taller women, knee length trench coats.

As for shoes, sandals, flats and even sneakers reflect the easy and more informal nature of this style. But heels, particularly platforms and heeled sandals, work better with more classical pieces above the waist.

Apple Shaped dressing: Since you Apple ladies tend to have a nice bust line, work it! Look for either scooped or V-necks (depending upon which ones work for you based on your bone structure) and A-line or Empire waist tops that end a little below your hipbone. If you're wearing something like boyfriend jeans (sometimes a challenge for Apples) and really want to camouflage your waistline a slightly looser tee or sweater that is asymmetrically a little longer in the back than the front can create a nice silhouette for you. But be sure to keep the texture and weave of the material more refined than chunky and avoid large or wild patterns.

Peplum tops can visually create a waistline for you (just make sure that you can carry off this style — these work best for women with either the Romantic, Youthful, or Lively style type.) For jackets, single breasted Blazers and straight hanging cardigans deflect the eye from a wider waist.

You tend to have great legs. Okay, so jeans cover-up your legs. But you can still draw attention to them with the right shoes: nothing too dainty, nothing too chunky. Look for boots of many heights — ankle boots, lace ups, knee highs as well as more substantial sandals, both in flats and heels. Simple pumps work for almost everyone but if you want to draw more attention to your legs make sure they have something that stands out in color, texture or style. Espadrilles and wedges with a medium height heel are also nice on Apples.

For accessories, Apples do well by keeping it simple. And chunkier earrings, rather than delicate long hanging ones, often work best, as they draw the eye to the upper part of your body. Bracelets and cuffs, because they hang below the waistline, draw attention to your legs, which is a better thing than eclipsing your nice cleavage with large bib-style necklaces.

As for handbags, keep in mind that wherever the bottom of your handbag ends, that's where the eye goes. So, just look at yourself in the mirror when you're holding your bag. Shoulder bags can work for you as long as they don't end up too close to your hip line. You also don't want anything really big ending at your waistline. A more traditional style handbag that you carry over your lower arm can also work as can totes with longer handles that are proportionally sized to your body. The only one you might want to avoid is a cross body strap that covers up your chest. A flat clutch often works well for you, particularly worn with jeans and heels.

Flute shaped dressing: As you've already read in the Flute body type section, there are tons of options of jeans for Flutes and that also goes for how you can style them. But as was also indicated, there are many different types of Flutes based on height, muscularity, and whether or not you have some curves in your bottom or bosom. Generally we'll be looking at how to style a body whose vertical line from shoulder to waist and hips is fairly straight up-and-down.

For tops think fitted, tucked in, and wrapped — anything that emphasizes your body, creates a waist, and breaks up the line from shoulder to hips. You don't want to wear voluminous amounts of fabric that eclipse your entire torso. Opt for heavier knits and ribbing rather than flatter weaves. Sleeveless tops (they bring attention on your shoulders), three-quarter sleeves or rolled cuffs (they break up the vertical line), V-necks, and halter tops (exaggerate cleavage), and surplice or wrapped tops (that emphasize the bust line) work well for Flutes.

Wearing color in your tops can add a sense of volume. Try to avoid neutrals unless you have a patterned or colorful top underneath. Details like ruffles, patch pockets, and pleating also add some volume to your bosom.

Flutes can wear so many different kinds of jackets! Moto jackets with lots of detail like zippers are one great option for you. You can wear them cropped, waist length, or slightly below your waistline, particularly if you're wearing something tucked in underneath. Just try not to wear puffy or full jacket that ends meet the hip line if you have a disappearing bum. Blazers that indent on the waistline are best for flutes as are V-neck peplums. Shorter, chubby jackets are also a lot of fun. Straight up-and-down blazers or jackets pair best with fitted rather than bootcut or flared jeans.

Layers are definitely your friend. A fitted sweater or tee under a bulky or chubby jacket is a fun option. And don't be afraid to add a belt over a jacket. In fact belts of many kinds — from skinny to wide — (depending upon the length of your torso) work well on a flute shape body.

Ankle boots, with and without heels, mid-calf and knee-high boots bring attention and add shape to your lower legs. You're also one of the body types that can wear over-the-knee boots but if you're particularly thin avoid them as they can make you look emaciated. Simple pumps, elaborate sandals (both heeled and flat) gladiator sandals, sneakers, brogues, ballet flats — you can do them all.

Stacked bracelets, multiple strand necklaces, and more substantial earrings (that means anything other than studs or tiny hoops) are great for Flutes. Slouchy bags, totes, pouches, backpacks, and hobos are great for casual bag options. Satchels and Kelly type bags are better for more classic looks. You can also do a cross body messenger bag. Just make sure you pick the right size bag for your body: petite Flutes should avoid anything too big; and tall Flutes should avoid anything too tiny.

Hourglass shaped dressing: Styling an hourglass body is fairly easy because your body is already telling a story and you don't need to elaborate on that story too much. So, you can either play up or play down your curves depending upon how much of them you have. But always, keep it simple.

And above the waist, keep it fitted, i.e., avoid anything too shapeless. That means go for necklines that highlight your cleavage, including fine knit sweaters (you are the original "sweater girl" type) and tees plus wrapped and surplice tops. It's best when they are in patterns and fabrics that are a little more expressive of your more vibrant colors than neutral or toned down. In other words, work that body! (And do I need to tell you to make sure you have the right, supportive bra? Of course not. Every Hourglass practically lives in the lingerie department.)

Because you have breadth from your bust line, your body type can handle jackets with structured shoulders; that means slightly padded, one-button tailored jackets and blazers. Just make sure the blazers indent at the waistline and their hem is below the waist. That also means that cropped jackets are not the best for you because they visually scrunch down your torso. If the jacket has an exaggerated flare from the waistline, (such as a peplum) make sure the hem is close to your hip line.

Unless you're very petite, and assuming you can still wear them comfortably, high heels are a great option for an hourglass and can be worn with just about any style of jeans. Kitten heels also work well. Just don't go with ones that have an extreme exaggerated pointed toe. Generally rounder toes speak more of the hourglass shape. Anything with a peep toe also works for an Hourglass. For a more casual look ballerina flats or simple sneakers are more flattering than something like brogues. Short boots, fitted taller boots (not straight columnar ones), wedges, espadrilles, and wider-strapped sandals are also nice for Hourglasses. And chunky heels can work if you're wearing flares or if you're a plus size or a tall Hourglass.

In accessories, don't be afraid of a "statement" necklace that directs the eye toward your cleavage, as long as it's in proportion to your size. That means don't wear anything too prissy or "cutesy" above your collarbone, and avoid anything too large below it. You want to point to your cleavage, not hang a neon sign on it. Jangly bracelets or statement cuffs nicely draw the eye to your curvy hips (when your arms are down.)

Because you can emphasize your bust, waist and hips, almost any length bag will work for you. But try to avoid anything cross body that cuts across your curves.

Although curved shapes in handbags are favored for the Hourglass figure, and you can certainly carry something like a hobo or soft satchel, sometimes a square or rectangular handbag serves as a nice contrast that emphasizes your curves. The same goes for clutches: angled envelope clutches or pouches (for formal events) are options. Shoulder bags don't do much for you and particularly, avoid anything cross body that cuts across your curves.

Pear shaped dressing: Dressing for a pear shaped body is all about bringing the attention to your upper body, adding breadth to your shoulders, and grounding your outfit with statement or eye-catching shoes.

This means you can make your tops or jackets a focal point for your whole outfit. Structured jackets with some shoulder padding will give breadth to your upper body. You can even go with slightly exaggerated wide or larger lapels. But again, keep proportions in mind. If you're petite a wider lapel won't work for you. Jackets whose sleeves you can roll up draw the eye away from the hip line. The new long skimmer coats and trenches can be work very well for taller pears.

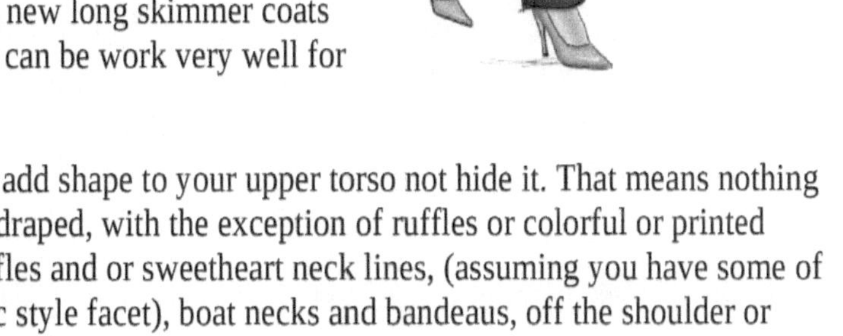

You want to add shape to your upper torso not hide it. That means nothing too loose or draped, with the exception of ruffles or colorful or printed scarves. Ruffles and or sweetheart neck lines, (assuming you have some of the Romantic style facet), boat necks and bandeaus, off the shoulder or capped sleeves, all these will draw attention to your upper body. Cowl necks and even large bows will do the same trick. V-necks that show a little bit of lace underneath are a sweet and feminine option.

Elbow or three-quarter length sleeves in lighter and brighter patterns and prints work well for Pears. That includes horizontal stripes. You can also wear sweaters with chunkier rather than fine knits. But pay close attention to where your tops end. It's best that they end between your waist and your hips. You don't want them to end right at your waist or be tucked in as that tends to emphasize the widest point of your hips in comparison.

Layering various textures, e.g. a looser chunky cardigan style top over a blouse or tee over a tank top, or a long (knee length or longer) outerwear piece over a more fitted top capped off with a statement necklace are great combinations for a Pear. If what's on your upper body broadens your shoulders and draws attention to your bust line a belted top or jacket (or a peplum jacket or top) will create a kind of Hourglass look.

But don't be afraid of belts or tops that emphasize your waistline. Depending on your size, you can even do a peplum jacket or top as long as it doesn't end at the widest point of your hips.

As for other accessories, larger chandelier or dangling earrings with a lot of bling are better than small and dainty hanging earrings or studs. Chunky, colorful statement necklaces look great on pear-shaped bodies.

In footwear, Pears tend to look better with somewhat pointed rather than round-toed shoes, but don't cram your toes into uncomfortable skinny heels! The idea is to elongate the look of your legs, and pumps of all heights will do this. Boots or pumps with thicker heels just peeking out from underneath bootcut jeans elongate the look of the leg, something shorter Pears appreciate. If you're wearing straight leg jeans avoid anything too delicate on your feet like strappy sandals. With straight or modified skinny jeans (nothing too body hugging) a platform heeled sandal, loafer or low heeled pump works better than a kitten heel or ballerina flat. A thick soled sneaker is also a good option.

Satchels and bowling bags that fit right under the arm or sling shoulder bags that end no lower than your waistline bring balance and breadth to your upper body. Just don't go with a cross-body bag that ends at your hipline. Envelope clutches are perfect for pear-shaped bodies.

Strawberry shaped dressing: All eyes will already be on your upper body and shoulders, so keep it simple above the waist. Avoid extras like pleating, ruffles, very bright or wild prints or tight knitted sweaters. A better way to show off your assets is with simple V-neck or round neck tees (depending on your face shape and style type) and sweaters in fine knits, and less tightly fitted classic blouses. Also, avoid anything that brings attention to your shoulders, such as shoulder pads or broad lapels. That means sleeveless and halter tops are not your best look. Also, avoid severe boat neck collars or patterns that cut you horizontally. They visually draw a parallel line to and emphasize your broad shoulders.

Generally, your jackets should hit below your waistline, particularly if you're wearing narrow jeans. Flare, A-line or peplum tops and jackets are very cute shape options for you. For a more classic look you can go with a collarless jacket or single breasted classic blazer with a narrow lapel. But make sure that they come in slightly at the waist, rather than hang straight down.

As with Apple-shaped ladies, your shoes are an important part of styling your jeans because you want to balance out your upper body and draw attention to something more substantial on your lower body. That means you can have a lot of fun with shoes. But avoid super high spikes. They will make you look as though you could topple over easily. Chunkier heels on your boots, (and you can wear all kinds of boots — ankle boots, Mid calf, or knee-high) particularly those with some kind of detail, e.g. zippers, stitching or embroidery, lace up, crisscross straps, or ruching bring a nice balance to your upper body. The same goes for sandals:

thicker straps on platform sandals create more ballast than thin strapped or dainty ones. Sneakers are fine too. And wedges or espadrilles in a low to medium height are another nice option.

You don't need a lot of neckline bling, but if you are wearing a necklace make sure that it is low enough to draw attention down toward your cleavage and not up to your shoulders. Anything too delicate or too heavy worn right around your neck brings attention to your upper body. (If you're wearing a delicate necklace keep it long.) So that means that bracelets, that automatically bring the eye toward your legs, are definitely a "yes" for you. Bangles or charm bracelets, or anything dangly work well for a Strawberry.

You can wear almost any kind of handbag — Shoulder bags, cross body bags, clutches, satchels, but avoid carrying anything that has to fit right under your shoulder. Having that much width so close to your upper torso takes the point of gravity upward again. Belts? Definitely! And that includes playful ones like fringed or studded — if your style types can handle it — particularly if they dip slightly in the front.

Everything Else You Wanted to Know about Jeans

Caring for your jeans

Designer Tommy Hilfiger swears he never washes his jeans. Designer Gareth Morris says he only has his dry cleaned. Manufacturer Levi Strauss suggests washing your jeans only rarely, and instead folding and then placing them in a zip lock bag overnight in the freezer!

Okay, so the (limited) research actually shows that not washing your jeans for up to 15 months doesn't create vast colonies of bacteria any more than regularly washed jeans does nor does it pose any health risks.

But honestly, it doesn't get rid of the funk factor. However frequently you choose to wash your jeans here's a simple sequence:

- **Remove everything from the pockets.**
- **Turn them inside out.**
- **Wash them on a cold setting.**
- **Line dry or on an air dry setting in the dryer.**
- **Iron…if you must…**
- **To retain a dark rinse or more saturated color, soak new jeans overnight in water with a quarter cup of salt plus gentle detergent; wash on a short, cold water cycle.**

When to Wear and Not to Wear Jeans

If you've read my book, *__Shopping for the Real You__*, you know that I am loathe to list a lot of rigid "don'ts." But being old school I feel compelled to set out some rules about when it is or is not advisable to jeans. Here's my personal list.

Weddings: only when the bride and groom are wearing them or if the invitation says "very casual attire."

Funerals: Just don't.

In the office: see job interviews below — know the culture of your workplace.

The opera: Really? Tosca? In jeans? Well, maybe Mozart would have if he were alive today. (You'll note I didn't write "the ballet" as a lot of young dancers go to the ballet wearing jeans.)

Most job interviews: living in proximity to Silicon Valley I'm well aware that this rule has gotten stretched to the limit, but still, even if the rest of the workforce is in jeans, a pair of casual khakis might be more appropriate for an interview.

Meeting "The Parents" or family for the first time: unless they all wear jeans all the time or the first meeting is at a barbecue, you might want to dress up a little more.

Religious services: probably okay if you're praying but not for formal events.

Other than that, jeans are pretty much fair game anywhere in public or private.

Age-appropriate jeans: I'm frequently asked what kind of jeans women over 50 should wear and there is a simple answer. Based on their individual body shape and personal style, older women should wear whatever the heck kind of jeans they want to!

Final word: Dressing for your body type is only one part of the equation of being authentic and looking great. It's also important to have a basic understanding of your seasonal color influences (yes, you read that correctly, plural: influences.) Almost every one of us has more than one seasonal color element reflected in our eyes, hair, and skin tone. The other part of styling is to understand how many style types your facial features, bone structure, height and body shape reflect.

All these elements are discussed in **Shopping for the Real You**, which includes a style type questionnaire to help you figure out how many of which styles you are. As far as seasonal coloring is concerned my own background is with the **Personal Style Counselors** color analysis system, so that is the one I recommend. I do not do color analysis myself, but here's a link to my mentor who has done color analysis for more than 27,000 people: **John Kitchener**.

Happy shopping for jeans!

Resource List

J ust about every design house and clothing chain produces a line of jeans these days, not to mention those from the ever-increasing number of premium denim manufacturers that keep popping up worldwide. As such, the vast majority of the brands and manufacturers listed here are US-based but ship worldwide. To track down all the international manufacturers would be a Herculean task.

The following list includes both the manufacturers and brands featured in the specific recommendations for each body shape. But, I've listed additional ones that consistently feature jeans as an important part of their business. What you will find here are descriptions of the kind of jeans each brand or outlet carries, the size range, and the price you can expect to pay for them. If you've heard about a brand and want to know if they might work for you this list is one place to start.

At the end of the list are a few manufacturers and retailers (without descriptions, but web-linked) who are known for offering jeans for specific needs: Petites, Plus, Tall, Maternity, Big Booty, Flat Butt, "Eco" denim, Bespoke, and Tummy Control.

When you troll a website be sure to check customer reviews, if available, for the specific pair that appeals to you. Most customers (except for those planted by the manufacturer, and you can't always tell who they are) honestly describe their body shape and how these jeans did or did not work for them. Sometimes that's the best way to determine if they will work for you.

7 For All Mankind: This is another one of the premium manufacturers that gets high marks and carries high price tags. They have a range of styles including wide leg flares from sizes 0 to 18 including some Petites and Talls. Their current signature is the skinny jean but their bestsellers are boot cut and boyfriend styles. They also have a line called "second skin" which is essentially leggings that really do look like jeans. The website offers a lot of **videos** that help you visualize how the jeans might look on your body. Medium-sized pockets with a fairly unobtrusive "swoosh" design.

Ag Jeans: Named for designer Adriano Goldschmied, these are another highly popular high-end option that works mostly for Flute shapes and sometimes Apples. They also have a pretty limited size range of 0 to 10, and mostly mid-to-Tall with the occasional Petite inseam. They offer skinny, skinny, cigarette, straight, boot cut, boyfriend, flare, and cropped styles. Interestingly enough, they also have a number of maternity sizes also in 0 to 10. Goldschmidt has also launched Gold Sign that seems to be a kind of experimental line featuring things that might not have mass appeal (e.g., really boxy boyfriends and high rise leather looking super skinnies that puddle around the ankles.)

Price Range: $160-$245

Alloy: This is a manufacturer that caters to everyone from juniors to Plus sizes with an incredible range (from 1 through 25) and offers inseams from 30 to 39 inches! You're bound to find something that fits. Skinnies, boot cut, flares, wide leg, trousers, hi waist for regulars, Petite, Plus and Tall – they've got it all going on. And they're cheap! We're talking $60 tops for almost all styles.

Price Range: $30-$88

American Eagle: Another manufacturer that primarily aims for the junior market but carries fourteen different styles including jeggings, skinnies, high rise skinnies, "Tomgirl" (oversize, low-slung, relaxed to tapered leg), straight, "skinny kick" (very slight boot cut), kick boot, "Boho artist flare," (distressed relaxed slight flare), "artist", (fit through the knee and narrow flare), "favorite boyfriend" (slightly loose boot cut), "fashion" (large square front pockets with a looser boot cut) and crops. Sizes range from 00 to 18; from short (Petite) to extra Tall.

Price Range: $40-$50

Ann Taylor Loft: The Loft carries seven different styles (cropped, skinny, hi waist skinny, straight, relaxed skinny, boot, boyfriend) and two fits (modern or curvy) in sizes from 0 to 20 including those sizes for Petites and Tall. Their curvy styles offer more ample room in the seat but generally their fits work best for Flutes and Apples.

Price range: $60-$70

Ashley Stewart: These are a godsend for Plus size ladies looking for well-fitting skinnies, flares, boot cuts and distressed jeans. Only complaint is that they didn't get the memo about how to size pockets for an ample bottom: theirs are awfully small. They have some Petites, some Talls, and all available in sizes 12 through 26.

Price range: $32-$60

Asos: Describing themselves as a "fashion marketplace" Asos carries thousands of styles from many different brands (already listed in this index.) But they also sell their own low-end label, in all the usuals including skinnies, flares, boot cut, boyfriend. Their Plus jeans have their own moniker: "Asos Curve." Sizes run from 00-28, Plus, Petite and Tall.

Price Range: $58-$68

Ayr: A newbie on the scene, Ayr offers LA-manufactured elegantly tailored clothing and very trendy denim available only online. They advertise "seven fits, five inseams and 20 washes." They describe their styles as "the ciggy," "the skinny," "hi rise wide leg," "hi rise skinny," "slouchy jean," and range from size 0 to size 16 and from a 26 inch (Petite) to a 34 inch (Tall) inseam. But it appears they have now added some Plus sizes. These are the low end of the premium market but high-end for style and quality.

Price range: $165-$195

Banana Republic: Well, not exactly known for the their jeans but these tend to get high marks for fit, particularly for Tall, curvy types and Apple shapes (although I'd rather see a higher front rise for Apples.) The same curvy fit comes in Plus and Petites. As part of the GAP group, (which includes Gap, Banana Republic and Old Navy) BR represents their higher end but still very affordable mid-priced product. Skinny, skinny ankle, boyfriend, flare in sizes from 00 to 16 (this is another one of the brands that manufacture large, so go a size down) in short (29 inches-Petite), regular (31 inches), and Tall (34 inches.)

Price range: $90-$110

Blank NYC: Blank has lots of contemporary, simple, well-made jeans in a variety of styles leaning toward a younger demographic. But unfortunately, they don't list their inseams for any of them. Some skinnies, some super skinnies, some deconstructed, a few boyfriends, the rare but wonderful trouser jean, in lots of different washes. Reasonably sizes unobtrusive pockets (but they don't show rear views unfortunately.) Limited sizes: 0 through 12.

Price range: $78-$98

Buckle: The US-based retailer whose primary focus is on casual wear carries an enormous range of jeans (more than 200 at last count) from six different manufacturers. They have three rises (low middle and high) and inseams from 29 to 37 inches from six different brands. This is not the place to find dressy jeans but if you're looking for distressed, feathered, embroidered, casual skinnies, straits, flares, and boot cuts they'll likely have something that works for you. Petite, Tall, Plus

Price range: $25-$240

CJ by Cookie Johnson: Born out of her frustration from trying to find jeans to fit her "boo-tay," Cookie Johnson, the wife of Magic Johnson, started this eponymous line with a spectacular launch in 2008 on Oprah's TV show. Her styles come with names like "Faith," "Wisdom," and "Glory" that generally equate to skinnies, boyfriends, and boot cuts, etc. Cookie gets the "rise prize" for those who have a little more bottom and who want to cover a little more waistline without going all "Mom jeans." Most have at least 8 ½" front rises with a higher rise in the back, guaranteeing that you won't be showing off a butt crack when you bend or sit. She also carries a lot of Plus sizes in mostly straight and boot cut. (I admit I'm intrigued by her roll-cuff pull-on ankle jeans with welt back pockets. They look pretty slimming and comfy.) Some Tall inseams (34 ½ inches.) Sizes 0 to 18 regular, and Plus size is 14 to 24. Currently they don't sell online but you can find them at mid to higher level department stores and often on sale via **Amazon.**

Price Range: $98-$205

Calvin Klein: Brooke Shields 1981 marketing campaign read "nothing comes between me and my Calvins." Those "skinnies" would be considered pretty tame in today's market. Now considered a lower end "premium" brand, Calvins are workhorse semi classic styled jeans, primarily offered in straight and skinny. In fact even their boot cut is so narrow as to appear almost straight. And their curvy style offers a nice higher back rise in waist sizes from 24 to 32. Typically dark washes and inseams of 30 or 32 inches they have a limited range but a loyal fan base.

Price range: $70-$80

Citizens of Humanity: Launched in 2003, Citizens has become a go-to for those seeking higher end premium jeans. They are always on the cutting edge of style and almost everything about them is super — super skinny, super distressed, super flare. Expect high quality material, high fashion, and high price tag. Curved yoke makes the butt look rounder and midsize but widely spaced, lower set pockets might not work for the well-endowed. Look for as many as 15 different cuts (including those illusive trouser jeans), three rises, five washes, Petite, and some Tall – 35" — inseams. And…maternity jeans!!!

Price Range: $168-$324

Chico's: A limited number of styles but they had to be included because of their ardent fanbase. These were the pre-NYDJ jeans that did not belong to your daughter. The only maddening thing about them is their size classification: 000-4, which translates from 0 to 20 (go figure.) Their styles are fitted but not super skinny, and all with higher rises, but not mom jeans, (except for one of the boyfriend styles) in slim, trouser, flare, barely boot, and a girlfriend ankle. With high, smallish pockets and a flattering seam next to the pocket that lifts the derrière. Tall, Petite and Plus.

Price range: $89-$219

Current/Elliott: This is one of the higher-end companies featuring a lot of very laid-back, often loose cut, more deconstructed-looking (lots of distressed looks) jeans particularly in their boyfriend and skinny styles. Pockets on the boyfriend jeans tend to be large low and saggy. Most of the others are fairly square shape with a pointed bottom, generally midsized. The flares, which come in a wide variety of washes, and some of the skinnies which have an enormous number of washes, patterns and colors, have a more pulled together, sophisticated look. Sizes 0 through 14, 30 inch inseams on skinnies; 34 inch inseams on boots and flares.

Price range: $198-$248

DL 1961: The advertising hype reads "we consider denim as a service." In that regard they offer cotton and lycra combinations with thicker 4-way stretch fabric that holds shape well. Their "instasculpt" series promises to hold in legs, butt and tummy. And, God bless them, they list Pear, Hourglass, Petite, slim, and curvy fits in boot cut, flare, boyfriend, and skinnies. Pockets are smallish and set fairly high and a curved yoke creates the illusion of a rounder perkier butt. Best sellers are distressed and "office" skinnies. Sizes 0 to 22. Maternity jeans too.

Price range: $168-178

Diesel: Kind of tough, kind of tight and kind of expensive, Diesel Premium denim is a UK-based manufacturer featuring high-end materials and the usual suspects (Boot-cut, skinny, super skinny boyfriend, flare and straight) Plus some edgy coated jeggings and super skinnies with multiple hip and ankle zippers. Smallish angled pockets except for their boyfriend jeans which have huge butt-dragging ones. They also have a wide range of jeggings and one maternity style in their "ergonomic" fit in mid to (mostly) low rise, sizes 0 to 10.

Price Range: $178-$325

Eddie Bauer: Not having had a reputation for being super stylish or hip, Eddie Bauer has recently stepped up their style game and has earned many a fan, old and new, for their consistency, clear descriptions, and illustrative photos: Truly Straight (straighter waist, flatter seat, smaller thigh); Slightly Curvy (evenly proportioned waist and hip, average thigh); Curvy (smaller waist, fuller hip, fuller thigh); Boyfriend (evenly proportioned waist, relaxed hip, relaxed thigh.) Their StayShape jeans get high marks for doing just that. All are available in short, long, Petite, Tall, and Plus sizes, all in mid to slightly higher rises

Price Range: $70-$90

Express: Those of us who grew up on Express (and similarly, the Limited) carry a soft spot in our hearts for this mostly juniors-focused company. But Express has certainly burnished their image with a very wide selection of stylish and contemporary jeans that will appeal to many demographics. Leggings, (honestly, these really just look like skinny jeans to me) girlfriend, boyfriend, flare (including sailor- type button flares), skinny, and "skyscraper" provide some pretty fierce looking options. Mostly midrise, some pretty low rise, and just very few high rise, in sizes 00 to 18 (Plus), in regular, Petite, and Tall. Fairly low pockets, some with a swosh-y design work best on small to moderate size bottoms. Some terrific sales.

Price range: $69-$228

Forever 21: True to their demographic, they are quick to bring out the latest trends at affordable prices for the junior to early 20's shopper (although you'll find a lot of happy older women finding bargains here.) Lots of high rises lately, several distressed ("destroyed" is more like it) skinnies and boyfriend or "girlfriend" jeans, lots of ankle skinnies, high rise flares and even one actual bell-bottom (!), Plus mom (why would a junior want mom jeans?) and bootcuts. Sizes range from zero through 12; very large selection of Plus styles in sizes 12 through 20, a few Tall inseams.

Price Range: $8-$35

Frame denim: A high-end US and UK-based company that carries mostly skinnies Plus a few boyfriend and flares, Frame jeans get high marks for their comfort. You can buy from their website but they're available from Nordstrom's, Neiman's, and a lot of the online sites like Blue Fly and ShopBop. Sizes range from 00 to 12 but customer reviews say they run large. Simple, small to medium pockets and fits that work best for Flutes and Apple shapes.

Price range: $198-$238

Free People: geared to a younger crowd, their jeans, like the rest of their brand, will certainly never be considered boring. They'll usually be found on the cutting edge of style, e.g., this year's flares. Sailor flares, embroidered flares, seamed flares, super flares, vintage extreme flares are a few of the current offerings. And in keeping with current trends, some high rises among their skinnies. Just a few boyfriend jeans, but they are notable for their more body hugging fit. Wide range of prices including some Levi's. Good customer reviews. Sizes 2 through 12.

Price range $78-$298

Gap: Having practically dominated the "fashion" denim era for decades (before the premium houses came on the scene) Gap has now been given a run for their money by many of the lower end fashion houses like H&M, Forever 21 and Zara. But, their fans are legion and they are one of the few manufacturers that still make some 100 percent cotton jeans. (These work in their "girlfriend" fit when you don't mind that they get saggy within a couple hours of wear.) Except for some of their 1969 skinnies which have 2% Spandex many of their styles have 1% Spandex. Skinnies, flares, boot cut, girlfriend, straight, and their Resolution 1969 series featuring some leggings and some interesting details that look like leather jacket stitching

Plus lean and curvy in short, regular and Tall. No embellishments on pockets so with darker rinses your bum will look smaller, but they're pretty large pockets. And their girlfriend jeans feature those large packets hanging past your butt. Sizes: 00-20; waist; 24-35.

Price Range: $70-$90

Genetic Denim: A favorite of Hollywood fashionistas this company is from (where else?) Los Angeles. They carry carries on trend, high quality regular and distressed skinnies and crops, boots and "bells" (flares) all in mid to high rise. Fairly low, fairly large pockets. And, maternity! Sizes 2 through 18, some Tall's.

Price range: $185-$390

Gloria Vanderbilt: Got so many comments from readers that they love their GV jeans even though a lot of their styles are dangerously close to Mom jeans. Expect to find some higher waists and looser legs. Pockets are midsize and placed high, giving a great butt lift. And, they have sizes galore from Petites, Misses, Misses short (cut larger than Petites,) Tall, Curvy, and Plus. But pay very close attention to size, and to customer reviews. Depending upon where they are manufactured size varies dramatically. Available at most of the old school affordable chains **JCPenney, Kohl's, Sears, Belk,** Plus occasionally, Costco.

Price range: $40-$46

Guess: This brand has mostly been known for their "spray on" jeans, and as such has been favored mostly by the younger, very thin set. These days you'll also find some bottom flattering curvy styles as well. They come with names like Power Skinny, Power Curvy, Pencil Skinny, Push-Up, Shape up, Curvy Acts, Rocket, Moto, etc. Still, you're mostly looking at skinnies and a few boyfriend in boot cut styles. Their "biker" jeggings don't look very different from their skinnies, except for the somewhat fierce stitching and horizontal zip pockets. Pockets vary by style so look carefully. Lots of good customer reviews Most rises are available but a large number of styles have fairly low ones. Sizes 2 to 12.

Price range: $80-$238

Henry and Belle: Named for the founders, Henry and Belle Mann, this Chicago-based mid-to high-end manufacturer produces a curated (i.e., limited styles and fits) series of well-made jeans, with couture sensibilities. They say some have a "contour" waistband, but they appear mostly low rise and designed for more flute shaped bodies. Flares, skinnies and bootcuts and angled, small-ish pockets. sizes 0 to 16 including some Tall inseams. (A portion of all their sales go to one of six charities — you choose.)

Price range: $128-$172

H&M: Like Zara, expect their styles and fits to be in one door and out the next quickly, so if you see something you like you may not want to hesitate. Didn't see much in the way of contour waistbands and they show very skinny models, so these will likely work best for flute shapes. Semi large, angled rear pockets in skinnies, straits, boyfriends, flares, high mid and low rises, and even some new "shaping" super stretch styles in sizes from 0 to 18 and in inseams from 30 to 36 (Tall).

Price range: $20-$50

Habitual: Founded in 2001, this was once an uber trendy, very high-end manufacturer. But now you will find some incredible deals on Amazon or ShopStyle. They feature mostly rock 'n roll skinnies and straight-leg jeans. Some of their rear pockets still have the distinctive iron cross "H" stitching but the newer models now simply have a very subtle "H" on one corner. The higher rises may work for a slightly curvier body. Generally longer inseams (Tall) in sizes 0 to 14.

Price range: $57-$242

Hudson: is a premium brand with an expanded version of the usuals: super skinny, skinny, straight leg, baby boot, boot cut, flare, boyfriend, cropped. In addition to regular inseam they carry what they call "Petite" (31 inches – and if you are a real Petite, spare me) a "ballet" (32) and a Tall "supermodel" (36.) Their useful fit guide shows front side and back views of each type but sadly they ditched the videos showing how they fit on a real person. Most of their styles have fairly large wide set pockets. Sizes 0 to 16.

Price range: $195-$265

J Brand: not only carries all the usual suspects but they also carry trousers and a large variety of maternity jeans. (Those have an extra low front rise and stretchy side panels for comfort and support.) With — for one example — a mix of 77% cotton, 21% polyester and 2% elastane you should expect longevity and retained shape. Sizes 0 to 12, several 35 inch inseams (Tall) and a couple of Petites.

Price range: $228-$248

J.Crew: Skinnies, high rise skinnies, straight, boyfriend, and cropped Plus a flare or two (including some cropped flares) are the usual fare at J.Crew. True to the brand they are almost always simple in design without much fanfare or bling. This is, after all, a company that leans heavily toward "preppy." Mostly for flute and apple shapes. Their Reid Cone denim is also available in Petite and Tall sizes. Sizes 0 to 12. Price variation is because they carry some lines in addition to their own brand.

Price range: $90-$198

James Jeans: Lots of options here for Skinnies, pencils, boyfriends, straight, boot cut, ankle Plus curvy and maternity. Their wide set, low pockets that angle downward work best on those with smaller bottoms who want to add some width or breadth. They feature lots of long inseams for Talls, lots of fairly high rises. Their curvy styles come in sizes 12 to 26 and they have a pretty cool boyfriend maternity style (all the maternity styles are pull-on.)

Price Range: $128-$194

Jag Jeans: Mostly known for the original pull-on jeans, they get good reviews for comfort. But they have added some traditional styles too. You're not going to find a lot of the trendier bells and whistles. What you will find is very serviceable midrise slim, boyfriend, ankle, cropped, and boot cut in sizes 0 to "L", which I guess is their way of saying Plus. But they indicate Petite and Plus sizes as well. Because they style many of them with tops covering the waist it's hard to see the pitch but I know the pull-ons work well for hourglass and pear-shapes. Available on their website or here on **Amazon**.

Price range: $53-$80

Joe Fresh: Another chain appealing to the H&M, Uniqlo, and Forever 21 shopper, they have a simple and inexpensive list of jeans. Boyfriend, slim boyfriend, highrise, classic, "jegging" (sure look like skinnies to me) and slim come with no bells and whistles, in very limited sizes (4-12) and medium-sized square pockets on the backside.

Price range: $25-$39

<u>Joe's Jeans:</u> Joe's jeans have earned an army of loyal customers for their stylishness and fit. And they have a humongous range of fits and styles. Apples, Strawberries, Pears and even some Hourglasses rate them highly. They carry skinny, boot, boyfriend, (shredded and pricey) cropped, ankle, straight, high rise, some Petites, curvy boot cuts and a very on trend "Collector's Edition." Pockets tend to be small, high and wide set. Sizes 0 to 14, some Petites and Talls.

Price range: $178-$298

<u>Jordache:</u> Sarah Jessica Parker, as their new spokeswoman, has just breathed new life into this old workhorse. Yes, they're still in business and making jeans at two price points: very affordable jeans available at <u>Walmart</u> (and carrying both Petites and Plus sizes as well as regulars) and then their updated line (the one that SJP advertises) that features a premium and a "vintage" collection of skinnies and mom jeans (yes, they actually call them this - and it's an apt description) at mid-level prices. Those would likely fit an hourglass or pear-shaped body best.

Price range: $10-$20 (Walmart $108 on the website)

<u>Kohl's:</u> No, they are not making their own jeans (at least not that I know of) but they offer such an enormous range of sizes — from Petites and Plus Petites to every size of regular and Tall — from a wide range of manufacturers that I had to include them here. Expect to find Levi's, Vera Wang, Jennifer Lopez, Lee's, Rock and Republic, Apartment 9 Croft and Barrow, Gloria Vanderbilt and probably some others by the time you read this.

Price range: $25-$88

<u>Kut From the Kloth:</u> This is a low end of mid-priced jeans company offering skinnies, boot cut, flare and a "relaxed" skinny in a variety of washes from sizes 0 to 16. Pocket placement (and you won't find pictures of them on their website, alas) is mostly wide but their sizing and stitching is all over the map. Some are completely plain, many have their curvy "V" insignia, and then there are few with flap pockets. They describe three rises, but they look mostly mid-to low in sizes zero through 16. Shop carefully. You'll find a bunch of them at <u>Macy's</u> and their website sales feature some styles as much as 60% off.

Price range: $90-$100

L.L. Bean: The venerable Freeport, Maine establishment has been serving up workhorse jeans for more than a century. But to their credit they've also stepped up their fashion game, offering some more stylish alternatives (midrise straight leg and boyfriend jeans) to their original Double L jeans which, frankly, will read as "mom" jeans on anybody. (If you *really* want a very high waist and roomy hips these are your jeans.) Their True Shape Jeans are more universally flattering. And they consistently get high ratings from their loyal customers. And if you're looking for flannel lined, look no further. Regular, Petite, Tall and Plus sizes – they've got it all. And of course, their perennial free shipping is a boon.

Price range: $40-$79.

Lands End: After decades of being considered the poor sister to J.Crew and a wannabe L.L. Bean, Land's End spun off from an unsuccessful several year alliance with Sears, nabbed former Dolce and Gabbana exec Federica Marchionni as their new CEO, and is now becoming a go-to brand for those seeking stylish jeans. Skinnies, slims, straight leg, boot cut in trousers in elegant dark rinses for regulars, Petites, Plus and Tall. What's not to love? Available in sizes 2 to 18; 16 to 26W. Pockets are reasonably sized but slightly wide set. High rise (in the straight leg version they're a little "mom-sy") mid-rise and their "not too low" rise.

Price range: $59-$69

Lane Bryant: They have been so crucial in providing stylish and current Plus size clothing. (And quite frankly, some of the most stylish women I have ever known are Plus size.) In addition to their regular jeans they have those with extra tummy control and offer boyfriends, skinnies, straight, boot cut and flares including some of Melissa McCarthy's 7 Seven Brand, available in Petites, Short and Talls, sizes 14-32.

Price range: $59-$89

Lee's Jeans: *"What Not to Wear"* maven, Stacey London, has become a spokeswoman for the brand so there's likely decent vetting of the sizes. Tall, Petite, Plus, Tall Plus, Petite Plus, curvy, "side in elastic", sizes 0 to 30, and straight, tapered, boot cut, "roll up", and skinny — you name it, they've got it. Terrific sales on their website; limited inventory but great prices on Amazon.

Price range: $40-$62

<u>Level 99:</u> A mid-priced new kid on the block, this company has a huge variety of styles and fabrics including an "eco-" denim and a "hybrid denim" that looks like jeans but feels a little like sweat pant fabrics (yes, I know I'm going off the "strictly denim" reservation here.) And they advertise themselves as "carbon conscious" which means they buy carbon offsets. Fairly wide and low set narrow pockets have a stitched insignia pointing downward. They carry more than a dozen styles and eight standard cuts (their "Sasha" boot cut and some of the high rises could work for an hourglass or pear) but most of these are for skinny flutes. Sizes 0 to 16 on their site and some on **Amazon**.

Price range: $115-$135

<u>Levi's:</u> They deserve a category unto themselves. Not only are they the oldest jeans manufacturer but they are the most consistent in terms of quality and fit. They've also led the pack in the area of sustainability and responsible manufacturing. In addition to offering Plus sizes (16 to 24, many with tummy control), Petite, Tall (up to 36" inseams,) and juniors as well as low, mid, and high rise, they have four categories of curvy jeans from "Demi" to "Supreme." They even have a **"Discover your Curve" quiz** to help you specify what works for your body. Their slim and sleek "Revel" collection, with its double yoke, promises to "keep its shape and show off yours." And except for their "Made and Crafted" premium styles which can run you upwards of you're not likely to pay more than about $90 for their highest quality. Of course, if you want a pair of button fly you can choose your own fabric and stitching color made to order — for $400! Levi's rear pockets range from midsize to fairly large depending upon the style, and the double curve stitching adds some roundness to your bottom, making them a slightly less attractive option for someone with very wide hips and a big bum. But they are also fairly high-set, visually elevating the cheeks.

Price range $44–$118

<u>Long Tall Sally:</u> This is a fashion website devoted to fashion for Tall women and their jeans section is the most extensive I've found for them. They carry their own brand but as an international website they feature ten other brands including Silver, Foxy and Second Denim. Inseams start at 34 and go up to 38 inches. Lots of skinnies, straight, boot cut, some boyfriend, flare, cropped, wide leg and maternity. Maddeningly, they

don't indicate the inseams on the examples. But you can click on inseam section in the sidebar to find styles in your leg length. (The sidebar only shows up to 38" but based on the reviews, they had some that were up to 39.") Sizes 4-20. Frequently have some great sales.

Love Nation: As with ZCO, which is also sold at JC Penney, these are inexpensive brand that caters Junior's market. They have very elaborate embellished embellishments — even on the larger sizes – and I have to think a lot of that bling is going to be uncomfortable to sit on for any period of time! Sizes 4 to 16, also in Petite.

Liz Claiborne: Ms. Liz has been on many an Apple, Hourglass and Pear's go-to list for years because of her high rise and contoured waist (big on comfort, occasionally in the "mom jeans" territory.) But their new "City Fit" adds some contemporary options in skinnies and boyfriend styles. Huge variety of sizes: misses, Petites, Tall, Plus, Tall Plus, curvy in sizes 2 through 20. Sold primarily through JCPenney.

Lucky Brand: jeans rank high on a lot of surveys for style and fit. Available in low, mid, and high rise, for Talls, Petites and Plus in sizes 2 through 16, (and up to size 28 in their Plus and Petite Plus sizes.) You can shop by fit (12 of them) leg (skinny, straight, boyfriend, boot) or rise (low, medium or high.) Plus size styles and in their "Curvy" fit they offer a contoured waistband that will work for Hourglasses and Pears. Lots of different color washes.

MAVI: They're still not very well known, but they probably should be, if only for the variety of sizes and simple, well-tailored fits in skinnies, straights, boot cut, relaxed boyfriends, and flares. The sidebar on the site is terrific: you can click on everything from "under $100" to "party wear" to "embroidery" to specific inseams. Square-ish, if slightly low pockets, they carry inseams in Petite 28" to Tall 36" in waist sizes 24 through 34.

Madewell: Heavily leaning to a younger demographic, they carry flares,

straights, skinnies, boyfriends, blingless, with very large and low, square-ish pockets. Five styles — skinnies, hi rise skinnies, boots and wides, straight, boyjeans, something they call "rivet and thread," (selvedge edge) and maternity. They have one 10" rise (not for the short-waisted) but many feature their signature 8-inch rise, so that means they will likely fit a variety of body shapes, not just flutes. You have the option of "regular, short, Tall or Taller" inseams. Monogramming is also available. Love the fact they show some Plus size models. Waist sizes 23"-35"
Price range: $75-$148

Maurice: This site offers a wide range of straightforward, reasonably priced, well made jeans (from a few different manufacturers) in a wide variety of styles and in sizes 14-26; trousers, flares, boot, straight, slim boot, boyfriend, skinny and jeggings. And, they carry Plus sized jeans for Petites, regulars, Talls and extra Talls. Unheard of.
Price range: $29 to $100

McGuire: Currently available at mid-to-high-level retailers, LA Based McGuire is a fairly new premium denim shop. Waist sizes run from about 23" to 31" at mostly "regular" inseams. Their site claims they will go retail "soon" but I haven't seen it happen in two years now. You can find them at **Nordstrom**, **Anthropologie**, **Revolve**
Price range: $198-$268

MiH: A fairly new and very hip UK-based premium denim manufacturer with a vintage feel. Flare, straight, skinny, slim and boyfriend. Boyfriend jeans are in 100% cotton. Their 70's style "Bay" jean sells out quickly and has welt pockets, and all (except for boyfriend) have unadorned angled square pockets that can be small to large depending on the fit. Their inseams run 30 to 33 inches and they carry sizes 2 through 18. (I'm figuring MiH stands for "make it happen.")
Price Range: $225-$280

Miss Me: This is company caters to juniors and features dozens and dozens of blinged-out jeans in just about every kind of pocket embellishments you can imagine: Crystal starbursts, Angel wings, iron crosses, fleur-de-lis, flap pockets, embellished yokes, patchwork "fixes" for rips and tears, you get the idea. They're all very cute but available in only limited sizes (0 through 12) and fairly pricey for the young teen set.

Price range: $80- $120

Mother Jeans: Maybe this was named in response to "Not Your Daughter's Jeans" but you won't find any mom jeans from this company. (They have one section they call "Mother Superior.") Hip, high-end, and fashion forward, Mother Jeans is turning out skinnies, straight, flares, boot cut, and boyfriend in mostly mid to higher. Sort-of Petites, Plus some Talls: 29"-34" inseams. Sizes 23" to 32" waist.

Price range: $198-$268

NYDJ: Originally named Not Your Daughter's Jeans, they put out a survey to their customers who, I guess, didn't want to be identified as such and so they changed their name and branched out into active wear and casual tops. But basically, these are the go-to jeans for women over 40 who want enough stretch fabric to keep anything from jiggling. You'll find all the regulars — skinny, straight, flare, boot cut, ankle, boyfriend — and mostly with a higher rise. In some of their styles they seem to have gotten the memo about their pockets (which were a bit large.). At any one time they carry more than 180 different styles in regular, Petite, Plus, and Tall and in multiple color washes, sizes 0 to 18 regular; sizes 14 to 24 women's. They…just…fit. But, definitely size down.

Price range: $98 $234

NY & Co: This is a mid-to low and company in the same marketplace as H and M and forever 21 (but with a little more sophistication) that offers their "Soho" line of jeans in skinnies, boot cuts, boyfriends, and flares Plus a whole lot of leggings that, frankly, just look like skinny jeans. Tall, Petite, and curvy styles in sizes 0 through 20 (some interesting double yoking on the curvy styles.) Unobtrusive midsized pockets, mostly unadorned some with their signature horizontal line minimizes the look of the derrière.

Price Range: $65-$80

Old Navy: if you love your Gap or Banana Republic Jeans, you're going to find something here that works at a very affordable price, as they are all under the same corporate umbrella. Old Navy is the low end of the triumvirate but still offers great quality. Straight, boot cut, skinny, boyfriend, their curvy's are available in are available in 0 through 30 (Plus); short, regular, and long (35") inseams; Petite sizes 0 through 16;

mid-to lower rise, but not terribly low. But heads up Tall girls: their long inseams are only available online. Full disclosure: after trying on and researching hundreds of jeans I bought a pair of their original skinnies and absolutely love them. They have some great options for an Hourglass body.

Price range: $30-$40

<u>PZI</u>: Hourglass gals, especially those with a big booty, are in luck here! They really "get" you. And they recognize you come in all sizes: Petite, regular, long, and extra-long (up to 38 inch inseams for Talls.) Skinnies, boot cuts, and flares, in sizes 4 through 18. They certainly don't shy away from pocket embellishments, so if you want to say it loud and proud, these are your jeans.

Price range: $69-$89

<u>Paige Denim</u>: Established in 2005 by fit model Paige Adams-Geller, these premium jeans promise to "lift the derriere, lengthen your legs and slenderize your hips and thighs," some with their patented "Transcend" super soft fabric. Their "ultra skinnies" (with double zippered front pockets) are the most rock 'n roll of their styles which include skinny, straight, crop, boot cut, flare, and boyfriend Plus maternity. Size, shape and placement of the pockets varies with each fit and style (wider set in larger in the skinnies, for some reason) mid rises that are actually midrise and front pockets that are almost squared off, which work well for the well-endowed. Generally these work best for Flutes and Apples as they are ample in the waist and smaller in the thighs. Sizes 0 through 22, Tall and Petite.

Price range: $179-$259

<u>Pilcro</u>: This is Anthropologie's in-house brand. They carry all the usual fits — skinny and straight, cropped and ankle, flare and wide leg, boyfriend and relaxed in mostly mid and high rise. Some pockets are small and fairly high set; most are mid-to large and the boyfriend pockets are large and low. Sizes zero through 16 in regular, Petite and Tall.

Price range: $118-$178

<u>PZI</u>: Small waist? Big booty? They got you covered — literally. This is one of those websites that really gets it for ladies with curves and extra curves. And they recognize you come in all sizes: Petite, regular, long, and extra-

long (up to 38 inch inseams for Talls.) Skinny, straight, boot cut, trouser, straight and flare in short (Petite), regular, long and extra-long (Tall) in sizes 4 through 18. They certainly don't shy away from pocket embellishments, so if you want to say it loud and proud, these are your jeans. Available on their site and on **Amazon.**

Price range: $69-$89

Ralph Lauren: Long ago Ralph got the memo that there are many women in many sizes who can afford jeans at many price points. As such, he made jeans one of the staples of his signature and they are all simple, straight-forward, well-made in boyfriend, skinny, straight and wide leg. For each price category those jeans have a very different look and name. There are no specific Talls indicated, but many have a 35 inch inseam. The sidebar is also very straightforward — pick your size, your fit and your price. Pockets are a tad large, but not overly so. Sizes 0-20 as well as Petites and Plus.

Price range: $90-$750

Red Engine: There are a lot of higher end jeans manufacturers who put out a smallish selection of jeans. Red Engine had to be included because they got praise from a number of readers. These are mostly straight leg with some boot cut, a couple of boyfriend, a couple of curvy, one skinny "trouser," a couple of flares. They describe three rises Plus their "signature" rise, which looks pretty much like mid-rise. Sizes 25 through 30" waist, no inseams indicated. Mostly available at specialty boutiques and on **Amazon.**

Price range: $173-$188

River Island: is a British clothing company with a US affiliate that sells mid-priced jeans designed for a woman's body, (curvy waistband, contoured yoke, lots of higher rises) but alas, in a limited size range: 2 through 14. They offer Petite, Plus and Tall. Mid to smallish pockets and angled, minimizing the size of your derrière.

Price range: $80-$90

Rock and Republic: Sold through Kohl's, therefore reasonably priced, these get high marks for Flutes and Apples, although they also offer a curvy cut in boot cut, flare, skinny, and straight. Three rises, Petites, Talls and Plus, in sizes 0 through and 18 and women's through 24W. Small-ish angled pockets. Very frequent sales, often at almost half price.

Salsa: This European brand has a wonderful selection of mid-priced stylish jeans in unusual, but very practical and descriptive styles: slim, push-up, push in, comfort, hi waist, boyfriend, daughter, slim carrot, regular, curvy, flare, maternity, and "no gap" — apparently meaning hourglasses and pears might be in luck. Pockets are smallish and square-ish with an angled bottom, and unobtrusive except in some of the pricier styles for which they have a very cute pattern at the top of the pocket that elevates the bum. Lots of low rises but some higher ones (as is the current style — this too shall pass.) Sizes 0 through 16.

Seven 7 Jeans: Formerly based in Los Angeles, this company now makes its home base in Europe. Melissa McCarthy designed a new Plus size series for them. Skinny, girlfriend, boot and slim. Pockets are smallish but their embellishments are all over the map: swirls, satiny "V" shapes, bling. They also feature a lot of embroidery, bring and deconstruction. So choose carefully. Sizes 4 through 16

Silver Jeans: Silver has a terrific selection for regular and Plus sizes with inseams ranging from 22 to 37 inches (Tall), three rises, and three rinses Plus colors. Boot cut, baby boot cut, slim boot cut, skinny, straight, slim, pencil, boyfriend/pajama, flare (whew!) as well as Plus sizes that include straight, defined curvy, well defined curvy, slightly curvy and four different comfort levels of denim! With high set, fairly small pockets that have a swooshy "S" insignia on the back — nice for ladies who want to build up their derrière a bit. Sizes zero through 14 regular, 14 through 24 W. But heads up: reviews indicate they run small.

Simply Be: This UK-based Plus-size fashion company has an enormous selection of some really cute styles: straight, skinnies, boot cut, boyfriend, shape and sculpt, slim and wide legs and hi waist. Multiple washes, most available in sizes 6 through 32 and lengths from 27 (Petite) through 34 (Tall.) If you are Plus-sized or curvy, it's worth just looking at the site for all the empowering pix of beautiful, larger women.

Siwy: This is a high-end premium brand that works well for ladies with flatter bottoms who want their jeans to hug rather than hang. (But they also have a few curvy styles that flatter fuller bottoms.) Their curved yoke provides the structure for both ample and flat bums. Small-ish pockets, some with embellished stitching, work best for smaller bottoms. They have a maddeningly non-descriptive listing of styles ("Burning Bridges," "Nothing is Sound," "Starboy") but mostly skinnies, relaxed, bootcut, boyfriend and flareoffered in waist sizes 23-32 and in mostly regular inseams.

Price range: $177-$254

Skinny Jeans: Available in both skinnies and skinny boot-cut styles, these are built with design elements engineered to elevate your bum, thin-out your thighs and with a slimming contour waistband. Higher content of elastane than many brands. Their flexible waistbands deemphasize a wider waist (a great option for Apple shaped bodies.) Fairly wide, fairly low-set pockets. Waist sizes 24-38, up to 37" inseamsTalls and Petites, (the inseams run from 32-37".)

Price Range: $175-$188

Target: Well yes, of course they have more than jeans, but they have so many jeans from so many manufacturers that fit so many bodies I definitely had to include them. Skinny, Curvy, Flare and Maternity, Petite, Tall, Plus, you name it in every style, they've got it. And of course, they are all at extremely reasonable prices, including sale items that run under 15 bucks.

Price range: $28-$58

Torrid: is another juniors brand featuring an enormous range of styles for Plus sizes: stiletto skinny, lean, jegging, hi-rise skinny, curvy skinny, boyfriend, ex-boyfriend (!), barely boot, slim boot and relaxed boot. Available in sizes from 12 to 28, from extra short (read: Petite) to extra Tall, mostly higher rises, small-ish square pockets with no embellishments.

Price range: $59-$98

True Religion: A premium denim manufacturer founded in 2002 and boasting the Made in America seal. The aesthetic is 1970's inspired boho chic in skinnies, boot-cut, and straight styles along with Curvy Skinnies. Petites are available in boot cut. The U-shape insignia on square-ish mid-size pockets looks like a cattle brand (no comment) and some come with flap pockets that train the eye on your butt, a useful feature for ladies with flatter butts and/or smaller perky ones. Mostly for Flutes and Apples. Sizes 23-38" waist, 28-34" inseams.

Price range: $189-$331

<u>**Uniqlo:**</u> Yes, they don't have a big variety, but they've become an instant phenomenon. But they do come in a very wide variety of washes. They call their styles Skinny, Slim and Boyfriend. If you have much jiggle going on these are not the jeans for you. Extremely popular with the younger set, including juniors, and primarily for Flutes and Apples, they are an inexpensive staple. Sizes 0 through 12. Run a little bit long. Their sales and online sales are terrific, but specific sizes go very quickly.

Price range: all $39

<u>**Urban Outfitters:**</u> Very trendy, a changing list of manufacturers including their own Urban Renewal joint venture with Levi's. Because they cater to the Juniors market they have a pretty fast turnover of styles.These are mostly for Flute and Apple shapes. Pocket placement, shape and embellishments vary depending on the specific style, as does the price which varies wildly. Urban Renewal, ZeeGee and BDG (the last two are the most flattering) brands are the most inexpensive; the Neuw brand is pricier. Inseams 25"-33", 26-33" waist; mid to Hhgh rise.

Price range: $59-$178

<u>**Walmart:**</u> Well of course, Walmart had to be included, if only for the enormity of their selection (hundreds online) and the affordability of their prices. Brands include Levi's, Lee, Faded Glory, Jordache, Diesel, Tommy Hilfiger Plus a few others. You'll find boot cut, boyfriend, skinny, boyfriend, flared, "regular" (is there such a thing?) and trouser. Plus, Petite, and Tall. Some of their Faded Glory styles come in two-packs for $25. Sizes 6-20.

Price range: $15-$80

<u>**Wrangler:**</u> Founded in 1949, Wrangler has maintained its focus on jeans for the Western lifestyle including those for riding and rodeo aficionados, but has earned a huge fandom for their consistency, extensive size range,

quality, and affordable prices. Petites, Tall's, Hourglasses and Pears are likely to find something to fit here, as in addition to their regular fits they offer semi curvy and curvy styles (and Flame Resistant!!) in sizes ranging from 0 through 26 (Plus.) Low, medium and high rises. Lots of boot cuts and skinnies, but their straight leg jeans lean heavily toward "mom jeans." Stylized "W" stitching varies on different pockets.

Price range: $35-$119

YMI: is a low to mid-price Juniors size manufacturer that features their patented "WannaBettaButt" jeans, meaning the yoke, seaming, and fabric all lift and enhances the derrière. Skinnies boot cut and flare are available in Junior sizes 1 through 13, but they also list extra small, small, medium, large, an extra large (Plus) in Petites and Talls. Available on their site and **Amazon**.

Price range: $38-$58

Finally, here are a few curated listings for brands and sites that cater to specific body types or interests.

Bespoke Jeans: Design or clone your favorites

3x1/Bespoke
Denim Revival
Levi's
madetoorderjeans

Big Booty: Those precious few manufacturers who "get" what it means to have an ample and voluptuous bottom.

Ariya
Ashley Stuart
Ivido
Miracle body
Poetic Justice
PZI
Silver
Verox
YMI

Flat Bum: Fitted to emphasize every curve, and offer visual uplift. (Mostly for Flutes and Apples)

3x1
AG Jeans
DL1961

Hudson
Liverpool
Long Tall Sally
MissMe
Rock and Republic
True Religion

"Green" Jeans: For all eco denim fans who want organic and/or sustainable jeans

AG Jeans
Eileen Fisher
G-Star Raw
Kuyichi
Level 99
Levi's (yes! Levi's)
Monkeegenes
RECO
Second Clothing
Sonas Denim (recycled materials)

Maternity jeans: for moms-to-be!

ASOS
DL 1961
Destination Maternity
JBrand
James
Paige Denim
Salsa
She and Wolf

Petite: For those who are tired of paying the tailor for hemming

American Eagle (See sidebar for "short" length)
Citizens of Humanity
Gap
Land's End
Joe's
Lee
Levi's
NYDJ
Old Navy
Paige Denim
The Loft
Top Shop

Plus size: Fashionable and well fitting for sizes 14-28

Ashley Stewart
Avenue
JC Penney

James Jeans
Jessica London
Lane Bryant
Lee's
Levi's
Mynt
Poetic Justice
Salsa
Simply Be
Silver
Torrid
Walmart

Tall: Catering to ladies requiring jeans with at least a 34" inseam and longer.

Alloy
American Eagle
Ann Taylor Loft
BKE at the Buckle
Chicos
GAP
Height Goddess
Hudson
JC Penney
Levi's
Long Tall Sally
Old Navy
MAVI
Paige
Rock and Republic
True Religion
Silver Jeans
Skinny Jeans

Tummy Control (also check out the Plus size sites)

Gap (high-rise)
Just My Size
Lane Bryant
Lee's Riders
Levi's
Miracle Body
NYDJ
Simply Be
Style and Company